Contents

Introduction 6
A Sneak Peek 8
Governing for All 10
The Road to Independence 12
Creating a New Government 14
Shaping the Constitution 16
News We Can Use 18
Fitting the Bill 20
Close-Up: How to Make an Amendment 22
Even More Amendments 24
Rejected! 26
What the Constitution Created 28
Congress: Crafting the Laws 30
Head of the House 32
Really Remarkable Reps 34
Close-Up: How Many Representatives? 36
House History 38
Great Debate: How Long Should Members Serve? 40
Making Sense of the Senate 42
Some Standout Senators 44
Senate Moments 46
Great Debate: Bust the Filibuster 48
The Executive Branch 50
   Some Prominent Presidents 52
      Presidential Facts and Stats 54
         Hail to the Veep 56
            Going to College 58
               Great Debate: Do We Need the Electoral College? ... 60
               Ex-Executive 62
            A Set of Secretaries 64
            Presidential Partners 66
         Department Details 68
           Super Important Agencies 72
   The Judicial Branch 74
Supremely Important Decisions 76
Stars in Court 78
Federal Courts of All Sorts 80
How to Make a Law 82
Putting on the Pressure 84
A Capital Idea 86
That's Monumental 88
Great Debate: Should D.C. Be a State? 90
POTUS Is in the House 92
White House Fun Facts 94

White House History 96
Home Away From Home 98
Inside the Capitol 100
Not Just Any Library.........................102
Museums and More 104
On Display..................................106
Shh ... This Section Is Full of Secrets..........108
Join the Party! 110
Party People: Democrats....................112
Party People: Republicans 114
More Than Two Can Play...................116
On the Run 118
Bang for the Buck..........................120
Presidential Primary Picks...................122
It's Debatable..............................124
The Role of Polls 126
Time to Vote!..............................128
It's an Honor 130
States of Power 132
Go, Gov, Go!...............................134
Laying Down the Laws 136
Judging the States.........................138
Great Debate: Should Judges Be Elected?.....140
State Dos and Don'ts.......................142
They Can Do What?........................144
Voter Power 146
State Capital Ideas.........................148
Count On Counties 150
Local Motion 152
Whatta Job!...............................154
Fido for President 156
Officially Odd 158
There Oughtta Be a Law 160
Nations Within a Nation 162
Governing Native American Country.........164
Island Lands 166
People Power..............................168
Do Your Part! 170
Class Acts.................................172
Running for Real...........................174
Symbols of the United States 176
Test Your Knowledge 178
Glossary..................................180
Index.....................................184
Photo Credits..............................191

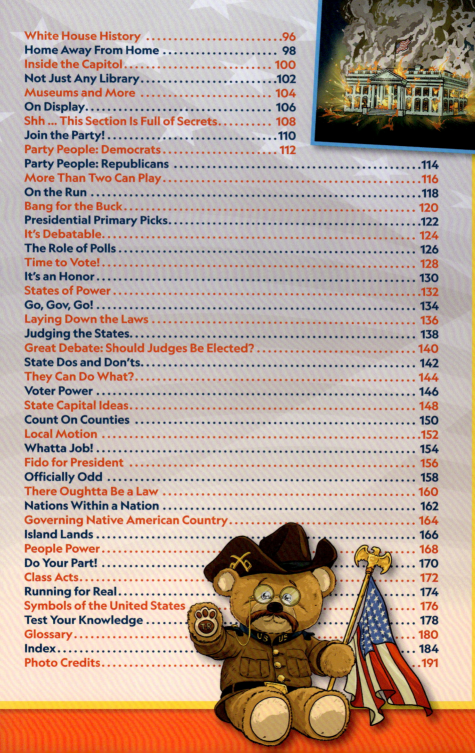

Introduction

UP UNTIL THE **1890s**, PEOPLE WOULD SOMETIMES **VOTE BY VOICE IN PUBLIC,** SO EVERYONE KNEW HOW THEY VOTED!

WHAT IS A GOVERNMENT, ANYWAY?

Simply put, a government is a system of rules that people in a certain group are asked to follow, as well as the people in power who make those rules. So at its most basic, a government is made up of the LEADERS and the LAWS.

Governments can be big or small. Some are ruled by kings or queens, while others are led by presidents or prime ministers elected by the citizens. Either way, they have changed a lot over time.

Around the world, many people believe that a government should help keep order by creating and enforcing laws, which means making sure people follow those laws.

Many people also want their governments to create and invest in services to improve everyone's quality of life. These include

★ keeping people safe,
★ providing health services,
★ making sure people have jobs and enough money for food and housing,
★ protecting animals and the environment, and
★ promoting ideas that the society values.

What are some of the ideas that a society might value? Many people believe education benefits citizens, so towns and states typically set up schools. Stealing harms citizens, so in most places, thieves face punishment, like time in prison, if they are caught and found guilty.

PEOPLE POWER

Who governs us? In President Abraham Lincoln's famous Gettysburg Address, he called the United States a "government of the people, by the people, for the people." Governing is about using power to achieve a goal, and since the United States was created, the vision for the country has been that power should begin with the people. American citizens use their power to vote for the leaders they want to hold government offices—from city mayors all the way up to the president of the United States. Once elected, these leaders have power. But they can't just do whatever they like. Just like everyone else, they have to follow rules!

Many American citizens also join political parties—groups of people who share similar ideas on what the government should do. The parties then try to get their own members elected to office.

Government and politics can seem confusing. After all, there are tens of thousands of governing bodies in the United States—from boards that run schools to independent governments among Native Americans (read more about tribal law on pages 164–165). In this book, we'll explore all the areas of U.S. government and how they work together for "We the People"!

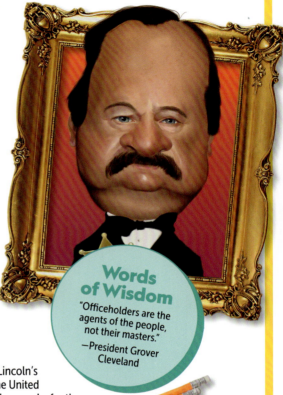

Words of Wisdom

"Officeholders are the agents of the people, not their masters."
—President Grover Cleveland

THE GOVERNMENT AND YOU

What are some of the ways government touches your daily life?

★ If you go to a public school, local elected officials make sure you have enough teachers and supplies.
★ If you play at public parks, people hired by your local government help keep them clean.
★ Your favorite foods are good to eat thanks to laws that prevent companies from selling unsafe items.

A SNEAK PEEK

Governing is serious business, but sometimes it can be weird and wacky, too. Here's a sneak peek at some fun facts about people, places, and ideas that you'll learn more about as you read on.

MONSTER MANAGEMENT

Most scientists agree that Bigfoot isn't real, but that hasn't stopped the Federal Bureau of Investigation (FBI) from creating a file about the furry phantom. FBI scientists examined some hair thought to be from Sasquatch (another name for Bigfoot derived from an Indigenous language). Learn more about the FBI, and the Justice Department's work, on page 69!

WELCOME (BACK) TO EARTH!

John Glenn was one of three U.S. senators who soared into space before heading to Washington, D.C. Learn more about the Senate and some of its members starting on page 42.

PRESIDENTIAL PLAYTIME

If bowling is right up a president's alley, they're in luck! Since 1947, during President Harry S. Truman's term, U.S. presidents have had their own private bowling alley. Learn more about the many benefits of living in the White House on page 92.

A MILLION DOLLAR IDEA … OR MAYBE NOT

What would you do with one million smackeroos? One lucky voter in Arizona almost found out! Voters had a chance to decide whether the state would award a million dollars to a random voter each election, in an effort to increase voter turnout. Learn more about how voters can call for and vote on new laws on page 146.

DON'T EVEN THINK ABOUT IT!

If you're in Los Angeles, don't even think about surprising your neighbor with a car wash. Sudsing up someone else's wheels without asking first is against the law. Take a look at more weird laws on page 160.

REALITY TV

The televised political event that drew the most U.S. viewers was a 2016 debate between then presidential candidates Donald Trump and Hillary Clinton. Presidential debates help voters learn about the people seeking the country's highest office and what they think about important issues. Find out more about the debates on page 124.

9

Governing FOR ALL

The United States covers a lot of ground—it's the fourth largest country in the world by land area (after Russia, Canada, and China). And more than 330 million people call it home. That's a lot of people to govern! To do it, Americans partially rely on what's called a federal system. This means the national (or federal) government, which is based in the country's capital of Washington, D.C., shares governing powers with the 50 states. The federal government creates and enforces laws that apply to all the states. Each state also has its own government largely based on the federal one (see page 133). The laws a state creates apply only to its residents. Local and tribal governments have similar features, too (starting on page 150).

As with all things "human," the United States is not perfect. But this work in progress sure has some good systems going for it!

WHAT'S IN A NAME?

The United States has a federal system of government. It is also a republic. A republic is a government in which the citizens choose representatives—like governors, senators, and school board members—to act on their behalf. In republics, voters hold the power in the government. If voters feel the officials they elected are not doing what they want, the voters can choose new leaders in the next election.

A republic has some pluses. Rather than holding an election for every proposed law, which would take a lot of time and money in a country as big as the United States, the idea is that, instead, elected leaders can represent the wishes of the people and vote on their behalf. In theory, republics can fix problems more quickly. But republics aren't perfect. Some Americans think wealthy people and groups can use their money to unfairly influence who gets elected and which laws are passed.

Some people use other names to describe the U.S. government:

Words of Wisdom

"The government is us; we are the government, you and I."
—President Theodore Roosevelt

10

★ **DEMOCRATIC REPUBLIC** The word "democracy" comes from the Greek *demos*, meaning "people," and *kratos*, meaning "rule." So, rule by the people. In a direct democracy, a democratic republic's purest form, voters decide what laws will be enacted—or put in place—rather than elected leaders. For a major decision to happen, just over half the voting population needs to be in favor of it. While some states do allow forms of direct democracy, the people who created the U.S. government, sometimes called the Founders, thought a republic would better protect the rights of everyone.

★ **CONSTITUTIONAL FEDERAL REPUBLIC** This mouthful of a name refers to a federal republic that is based on a constitution, a document outlining the structure of the government and the rights of the people (see page 16). Constitutions are created to protect people over time, even as politicians come and go. But that's not to say that laws can't change along with changing times (see page 22). In addition to the federal constitution in the United States, each state has its own.

IT'S ALL GREEK!

The roots of direct democracy go back to the city of Athens in Greece. Almost 2,500 years ago, voters there met in outdoor spaces to debate proposed laws. Then they each put a pebble in one of two containers—for or against the law—or voted by raising their hands. All citizens were expected to vote. If they didn't, they were marked with red paint, which let everyone know who was not willing to do their part! But not all Athenians could vote. Women, enslaved people, and foreigners were not considered citizens and therefore weren't allowed a say.

11

The Road to INDEPENDENCE

FROM LEFT TO RIGHT: BENJAMIN FRANKLIN, JOHN ADAMS, AND THOMAS JEFFERSON WRITE THE DECLARATION OF INDEPENDENCE.

THE DECLARATION OF INDEPENDENCE INCLUDES THE FIRST PUBLIC USE OF THE PHRASE "THE UNITED STATES OF AMERICA."

The United States didn't have to choose a republic as its system of government. There are other forms of government. For example, some countries are ruled by kings and queens. In fact, Americans might still be the subjects of a British royal ruler—and maybe playing cricket instead of baseball!—if they hadn't taken a bold step in 1776. Here's a quick history lesson on what happened back then.

A TAXING PROBLEM

In 1492, Italian explorer Christopher Columbus stumbled upon North America. In the centuries that followed, Europeans traveled across the ocean to colonize the region, and by the mid-1700s, Great Britain controlled 13 colonies in what later became the United States. Some colonies had a form of direct democracy called town meetings, which let voters weigh in on local issues. Every colony had a governor and elected lawmakers. But the colonists didn't have complete control. They had to answer to the lawmakers in Great Britain's parliamentary government and to the king or queen.

For decades, Parliament and the royal rulers didn't pay much attention to the American colonists—at the time, they were more focused on trade and wars in Europe. After 1763, that changed. The British wanted more money from the colonies in the form of taxes. Taxes are payments the government requires, and the colonists weren't eager to pay them. Some colonists claimed that Great Britain didn't have a right to collect new taxes, since the colonies weren't allowed to elect anyone to represent them in Parliament. But the British responded, *Yes, we do have the right to tax you!* In April 1775, fighting broke out in Massachusetts between colonial soldiers and British troops.

FROM 13 COLONIES TO ONE NATION

Even with guns blazing and cannons booming, many colonists did not want to break free from Great Britain. But by 1776, more had come to feel that the 13 colonies should declare their independence. Leaders from the colonies met in Philadelphia for the Second Continental Congress. (The first had been in 1774.) With the help of four other people, Thomas Jefferson wrote a document saying the colonies wanted to break free from the rule of King George III.

Jefferson described the main idea behind a republic, also known as a republican government: that the power to govern rests with the people. Americans would choose for themselves the kind of government they wanted and the government officials they wanted to represent them. And they didn't want a king!

On July 4, 1776, the Second Continental Congress voted to accept Jefferson's Declaration of Independence. Of course, they then had to win their independence on the battlefield in what has been named the Revolutionary War. It took several more years of fighting and the loss of thousands of lives, but the United States did it. In 1783, Americans officially won the right to govern themselves.

Fine Print

About 200 copies of the Declaration of Independence were printed in 1776, and at least 26 copies still exist. If you ever stumble upon one at a flea market, grab it—it could be worth more than eight million dollars!

Ka-ching!

CELEBRATING INDEPENDENCE ... A COUPLE DAYS LATE?

On July 2, 1776, the Second Continental Congress voted to break away from Great Britain. One person in attendance was John Adams of Massachusetts. In a letter to his wife, Abigail Adams, the future U.S. president wrote that July 2 should be celebrated with "Pomp and Parade ... Bells, Bonfires and Illuminations from one End of this Continent to the other from this Time forward forever more." But it wasn't until two days later that Congress approved Jefferson's work, which is why Americans celebrate Independence Day on July 4.

13

Creating a New GOVERNMENT

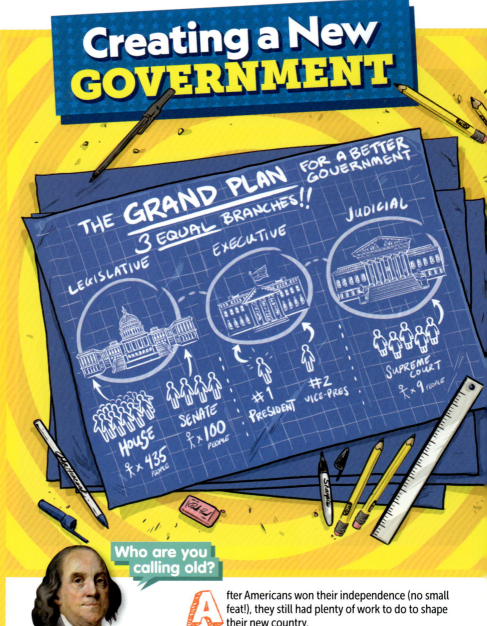

Who are you calling old?

Wise Guys
At 81, Benjamin Franklin was the oldest delegate at the Constitutional Convention. The youngest was Jonathan Dayton, at 26.

After Americans won their independence (no small feat!), they still had plenty of work to do to shape their new country.

During the American Revolution, the 13 states approved the Articles of Confederation, a document outlining the new national government and America's first constitution. But that government didn't have much power. The states were more like little countries that were good pals, with each wanting to do things its own way. By 1787, more Americans began to realize that their new country needed a stronger national government, one that helped the states work together rather than separately.

A GRAND PLAN

Representatives from 12 of the 13 states met that summer, again in Philadelphia, to give this new government another look. (Rhode Island liked the Articles of Confederation, so it didn't participate.) These delegates included Benjamin Franklin, George Washington, and James Madison. Together they decided that the new national government would be a republic, just as the individual states were, with voters electing others to represent their interests. The U.S. government would also become a federal system made up of three branches, or parts:

★ The legislative branch, which is the U.S. Congress, would make the country's laws and would be divided into two parts, the House of Representatives and the Senate.

★ The executive branch would make sure the laws that Congress made were enforced.

★ The judicial branch, which includes the country's courts (such as the Supreme Court), would interpret and apply the laws made by Congress.

The idea was to spread the government's power across the three branches—an idea called the separation of powers. Each branch would also have some ways to limit what the others did, a system of "checks and balances," so that no one branch held too much power. For example, the head of the executive branch had to approve any laws the legislative branch wanted to enact. And the legislative branch had to approve judges appointed by the leader of the executive branch.

Words of Wisdom

"I know of no safe depository of the ultimate powers of the society but the people themselves."
—Thomas Jefferson

Hard pass.

QUEBEC, CANADA, PASSED UP THE CHANCE TO BE PART OF THE UNITED STATES, BECAUSE ITS LEADERS DIDN'T LIKE THE ARTICLES OF CONFEDERATION.

Shaping the CONSTITUTION

I deserve a raise.

Not everyone was on board with what Madison and the others wanted. During a long, hot summer, the representatives spent sweaty days arguing over who would participate in the new government. Larger states wanted the number of representatives in the legislative branch to be based on each state's population, which would mean they would have more people in Congress fighting for things that would benefit their states. Smaller states didn't like that idea at all and wanted each state to have equal representation in each house. The solution:

JACOB SHALLUS OF PENNSYLVANIA WROTE OUT THE FIRST OFFICIAL COPY OF THE CONSTITUTION—BY HAND! THE JOB TOOK HIM ABOUT 40 HOURS, AND HE EARNED $30 FOR HIS WORK.

THE SIGNING OF THE CONSTITUTION

Hear me out, guys.

Party Poopers
Not all the delegates stayed in Philadelphia for the whole convention. Some returned home to work, while others left because they didn't like the Constitution.

Big states got their way in the House of Representatives (the bigger a state's population, the more representatives it gets), while small states got their way in the Senate (every state gets two senators—no more, no less!).

CONSTITUTION CONSENSUS

The debates in Philadelphia ended in September 1787. The delegates agreed on a federal, republican form of the new government and described it in the Constitution, the same one that guides the U.S. government today. The document was then sent to the states for their approval, which most gave in 1788, so the Constitution took effect. The Constitution left no doubt about who was supposed to run things in the United States of America. After all, it starts with the words "We the People."

Words of Wisdom
"A republic, if you can keep it."
—Benjamin Franklin, when asked what kind of government the Constitution created

NOT EQUALITY FOR ALL

Delegates at the convention argued over whether to count enslaved people when deciding how many representatives each state had in the House of Representatives. Several southern states that had high numbers of enslaved people wanted them counted, while states with few enslaved people opposed this. In the end, the decision was made to count each enslaved person as three-fifths of a free person. This Three-Fifths Compromise helped southern states gain seats in the legislature. It also showed that many representatives didn't see enslaved people as fully human. Slavery would remain one of the most explosive issues in the United States, leading to the Civil War in 1861.

News We CAN USE

Words of Wisdom

"Were it left to me to decide whether we should have a government without newspapers, or newspapers without a government, I should not hesitate a moment to prefer the latter."

—Thomas Jefferson

Don't forget about me!

How do Americans know what their elected leaders are doing? Today, we can get that information from the news aired on radio and television, posts on social media, and good old-fashioned newspapers. But in the Founders' day, the printed press—newspapers and pamphlets—was the main source of news. The press also gave Americans a way to express their views about what their elected officials did and what they would like them to do.

FREE ... TO A POINT

When James Madison wrote the First Amendment, he said a free press was a great defender of liberty. Newspapers needed to be able to write about or criticize the government, so voters could make good decisions on Election Day. But at the time, freedom to publish didn't mean newspapers couldn't get into legal trouble after they published something. That's still true today, as some laws let people sue the press or other sources of news in specific situations if what's written or said harms someone's reputation.

BY THE NUMBERS

In 1820, the United States had 512 daily and weekly newspapers. By the 1890s, that number was more than 13,000. In 2019, the number had fallen to about 6,700, as more people used other media to get their news.

FIGHTING DIRTY

How rude!

Soon after George Washington became president, some government leaders and wealthy Americans opposed his actions. Others strongly defended him. The two sides each had their own newspapers to express their views, which led to party presses—newspapers that did not try to be fair. Each wanted its political party and its candidates to win elections. For example, in 1800, a paper that supported Thomas Jefferson in his race against President John Adams called Adams hideous and "mentally deranged." Today, most journalists are instructed to cover politicians fairly and without inserting their own beliefs—unless they are writing an opinion piece. Most publications do, however, participate in a long held tradition of endorsing a candidate before an election, explaining why they favor one over another.

Fitting THE BILL

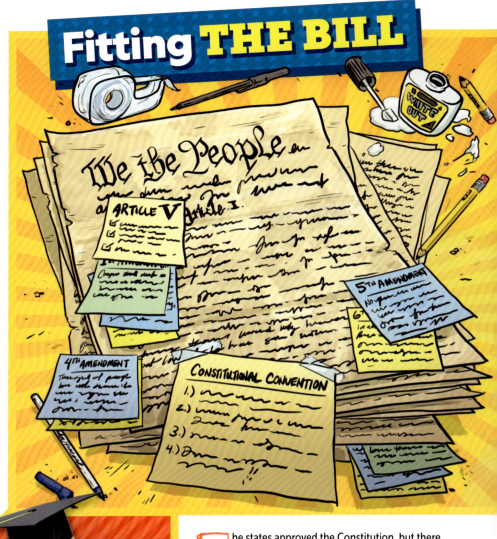

ONE OF THE TWO AMENDMENTS THAT WEREN'T PASSED IN 1791 FINALLY GOT APPROVED IN 1992— WITH THE HELP OF A COLLEGE STUDENT!

The states approved the Constitution, but there was still a bit more tinkering to do. Some Founders and other Americans thought the Constitution was missing a few things. They wanted a foolproof promise that the new government would protect certain rights. Not for all Americans, though, as women and enslaved people did not have the same protections at the time. The Constitution in 1787 favored the rights of white men who owned property.

To protect more rights, Congress approved 12 amendments, or changes, to the Constitution. By 1791, 10 of the original 13 states approved all but two of them, and those amendments are known today as the Bill of Rights. (As you'll see on page 24, 17 more amendments have been added since the Bill of Rights was passed.) Here's a quick look at the main points of each amendment in the Bill of Rights.

First Amendment: Guarantees the right to free speech and a free press, plus the freedom to follow any religion, to gather together peacefully in public, and to present concerns to Congress.

Second Amendment: Protects the rights of members of a well-regulated militia (civilian army) to keep and use guns.

Third Amendment: States the government cannot force people to let soldiers live with them in peacetime and can only require it in wartime if Congress passes a law allowing it.

Fourth Amendment: Prevents the government from searching a person's body or property without good reason and court permission.

Fifth Amendment: Ensures no one can be charged with a serious crime unless the government first presents evidence to a grand jury; no one can be charged twice for the same crime; no one has to say anything in a court that might get them into legal trouble; no one can have their "life, liberty, or property" taken unless all laws are followed; and the government must pay for any private property it takes for public use.

Sixth Amendment: Protects the rights of people accused of a crime to receive a "speedy and public trial" with a fairly chosen jury, to know the crime they're accused of, to hear the witnesses who speak against them, to present witnesses who can defend them, and to receive legal advice.

Seventh Amendment: Allows a trial by jury in federal court for certain civil issues, meaning cases brought by one private party against another, and prevents federal judges from throwing out certain verdicts in those trials.

Eighth Amendment: Bans excessive bail for people accused of crimes, as well as excessive fines and "cruel and unusual punishment."

Ninth Amendment: Asserts that the people have other rights not specifically spelled out in the Bill of Rights.

10th Amendment: States that the federal government has only the powers the Constitution spells out, such as collecting taxes or declaring war against a foreign nation. Any other power rests with the states or the people.

Know Your Rights

Ever hear that someone is "pleading the Fifth"? That means they're using their Fifth Amendment right to not say something in court that could be used to convict them of a crime.

THE RIGHTS LEFT OUT

There were two more amendments that the first Congress approved but that the states didn't. One outlined how many representatives should be in the House of Representatives, one of the two parts of Congress. The other prevented members of Congress from voting to give themselves a pay raise during the current session of Congress. In 1992, enough states finally voted for the second rejected amendment, and it became the 27th Amendment.

CLOSE-UP: HOW TO MAKE AN AMENDMENT

The Founders who wrote the Constitution knew their final document wasn't perfect—the desire for the Bill of Rights made that clear. When drafting the Constitution, the Founders included two ways for Americans to amend the original document. These amendments, or changes, could take something out or add something in.

The ways to amend the Constitution appear in a section called Article V (*V* here is the Roman numeral for five). And it's not easy! The Founders made it hard on purpose—they didn't want Americans to make changes to their work in Philadelphia without giving them a lot of thought.

BY THE NUMBERS

Today, 38 out of the 50 U.S. states need to ratify a proposed amendment to the Constitution.

PROPOSAL

1 CONGRESS LEADS THE WAY

2/3

In this first way of changing the Constitution, a member of Congress proposes an amendment. Then, two-thirds of the members of each house of Congress must approve it.

I have an idea!

2 THE STATES STATE THEIR IDEAS

2/3

The other way to amend the Constitution begins with the states, not Congress. The states can call for a convention just to discuss proposed amendments. To arrange this special meeting, lawmakers in two-thirds of the states' legislatures have to ask for it. States then send people to the convention to vote on the proposals. The proposals that get a thumbs-up go back to the state legislatures to be voted on.

THE PRESIDENT IS RESPONSIBLE FOR EXECUTING THE CONSTITUTION BUT DOES NOT HAVE ANY SAY IN AMENDING IT.

RATIFICATION

1 STATE LEGISLATURES VOTE

But the work's not done yet—three-fourths of the states must approve the proposal, too. They can do that in one of two ways: States can have their state legislatures look it over and vote yea or nay or ...

3/4

2 STATE CONVENTIONS VOTE

... they can call a special convention of delegates from the state to decide if they want the amendment. If enough states ratify, or approve, the proposed amendment, it becomes part of the Constitution. (This is the path followed to add the Bill of Rights!)

3/4

POWER TO THE PEOPLE

In either scenario, changing the Constitution is up to the people, through their representatives in Congress or the delegates they choose for a convention.

THE CALL FOR A CONVENTION

What would happen in a constitutional convention today? Nobody knows—Article V does not spell out the rules for a convention, and the country has never had one! While states might call for a convention to address one or two specific topics, because there are no rules, the delegates could propose just about anything they wanted. Some legal experts have worried that a constitutional convention could be dominated by groups with a lot of money to spend. They might try to shape new amendments to benefit themselves.

Balancing Act

As of 2022, 19 state legislatures had voted to call for a constitutional convention. Some were seeking an amendment to require the federal government to have a balanced budget, which means only spending as much money as it takes in each year.

23

Even More AMENDMENTS

Making changes to the Constitution might not be easy, but that doesn't mean it's impossible. Since the Bill of Rights was ratified, Congress and the states have approved 17 more amendments. Some of them have been huge—like the ones that ended slavery and gave more Americans the right to vote. Here's a quick look at the main points of these amendments and when they were ratified.

11th Amendment (1795):
Says legal cases in which a person from one state sues another state's government cannot be heard in federal courts, but in some circumstances can be heard in state courts. State governments sought this amendment to limit when they could be sued by citizens of another state.

12th Amendment (1804):
Changed how electoral college votes are cast, with separate votes for president and vice president. This amendment came about after a tie vote in the electoral college in 1800 created some confusion over who would become president. See more about the "college" on page 58.

13th Amendment (1865):
Ended slavery in the United States.

14th Amendment (1868):
Made formerly enslaved Americans citizens of the United States and their home state, and counted them as a whole person, not three-fifths; anyone born in the country is automatically a citizen of both their state and the country; states cannot deny the rights of citizens and must follow due process and treat everyone equally under the law; anyone who has taken an oath to defend the Constitution and then rebels against the government or supports its enemies cannot hold a government position.

15th Amendment (1870):
Guarantees the right of Black men to vote.

16th Amendment (1913):
Gives Congress the right to collect a tax on people's income.

17th Amendment (1913):
Allows voters in each state to directly elect their U.S. senators, instead of letting state legislatures pick them.

18th Amendment (1919):
Prohibited the sale of alcohol in the country, marking the start of what's called Prohibition.

19th Amendment (1920):
Guarantees the right of women to vote.

THE LONG ROAD TO THE VOTE

The 15th Amendment gave all U.S. citizens the right to vote regardless of their race, though some states still denied women that right until the 19th Amendment was passed in 1920. For Native Americans, the right to vote took even longer. Some states still did not consider them citizens who had a right to vote. In 1924, Congress passed a law that made Native Americans born in the country U.S. citizens. Some states, though, still denied them their voting rights. Finally, by the 1960s, all states allowed Native Americans to vote.

20th Amendment (1933):
Sets the end of the term of office for Congress members as noon on January 3 and the end of a term for the vice president and president as noon on January 20; makes the vice president the president if the elected president dies before January 20; gives Congress the power to choose someone to serve if both the elected president and vice president cannot take office on January 20.

21st Amendment (1933):
Repealed, or overturned, the 18th Amendment, ending Prohibition; gives states the right to set their own laws regarding the sale and use of alcohol.

22nd Amendment (1951):
Sets a limit on how many four-year terms a president can serve—just two. But a vice president who takes over for a president can serve up to 10 years.

23rd Amendment (1961):
Gives Washington, D.C., three electoral votes for presidential elections. To learn more about the special status of the capital city, see page 90.

24th Amendment (1964):
Prevents states from making voters pay any kind of tax to vote.

25th Amendment (1967):
Spells out who will take office if a president or vice president dies, is impeached (see page 62 for more on the process of impeachment), or resigns, and how the presidency is filled if a president is sick or otherwise can't carry out their duties.

26th Amendment (1971):
Sets the voting age to 18 for state and federal elections.

27th Amendment (1992):
Prohibits members of Congress from giving themselves a raise during the current legislative session.

So roomy!

Making Strides

Pants-like clothing called bloomers made it easier for women to move around, compared with the big skirts that were popular during the 19th century. Some women who fought for the right to vote wore bloomers as a sign of their independence.

IN 2018 AND AGAIN IN 2023, ONE LAWMAKER PROPOSED A NEW AMENDMENT THAT WOULD LOWER THE VOTING AGE AGAIN—TO 16!

REJECTED!

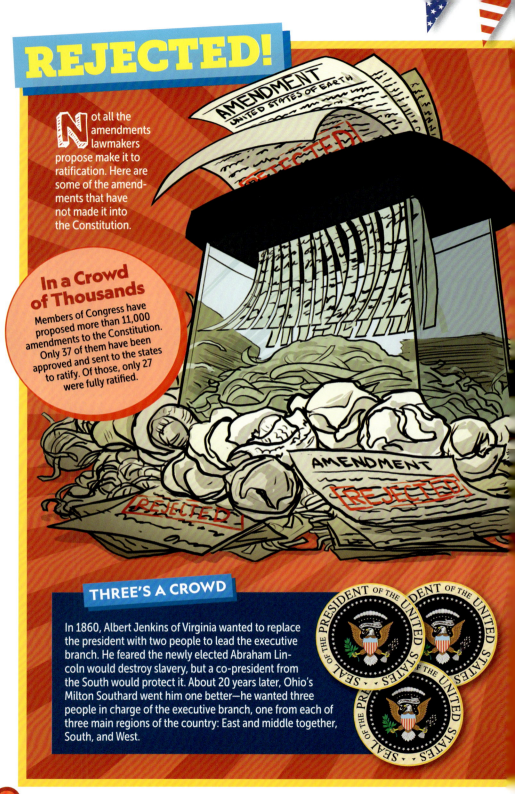

Not all the amendments lawmakers propose make it to ratification. Here are some of the amendments that have not made it into the Constitution.

In a Crowd of Thousands

Members of Congress have proposed more than 11,000 amendments to the Constitution. Only 37 of them have been approved and sent to the states to ratify. Of those, only 27 were fully ratified.

THREE'S A CROWD

In 1860, Albert Jenkins of Virginia wanted to replace the president with two people to lead the executive branch. He feared the newly elected Abraham Lincoln would destroy slavery, but a co-president from the South would protect it. About 20 years later, Ohio's Milton Southard went him one better—he wanted three people in charge of the executive branch, one from each of three main regions of the country: East and middle together, South, and West.

THINKING BIG ... REALLY BIG

In 1893, acting on a request from someone else, Representative Lucas Miltiades Miller of Wisconsin wanted to rename the country "the United States of the Earth." The reasoning: He thought the country could one day add every nation on Earth as a new state. Miller's amendment would have gotten rid of the U.S. Army and Navy, too.

STILL FIGHTING! THE EQUAL RIGHTS AMENDMENT (ERA)

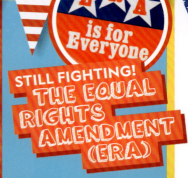

ERA is for Everyone

This amendment was initially proposed in Congress in 1923 and was sent to the states to ratify in 1972. The ERA would have made it illegal for the federal or state governments to deny equal legal rights to women. Congress set a deadline for states to consider the ERA. When time ran out, 35 states had ratified it—three short of the 38 needed to add it to the Constitution. Since 2017, three more states have ratified the ERA, but since those votes came after the original deadline, the amendment is still not part of the Constitution. Some supporters have fought in court to have those ratifications accepted so that the ERA can become the 28th Amendment.

TILL DEATH DO THEY PART?

Starting in the early 1900s, several lawmakers called for amendments that would limit a married couple's right to get a divorce and remarry. One idea would have banned divorce completely. Another proposal was to give Congress the power to pass laws that limited the right to a divorce.

SPREAD THE WEALTH

In 1933, the United States and the rest of the world were going through the Great Depression. Millions of people had lost their jobs, and some struggled to find food and housing. Representative Wesley Lloyd of Washington State proposed that the people who still brought in the big bucks should share the wealth. People who earned more than one million dollars per year (equal to about $20 million today) would have to turn over the extra money to the government, which it would use to pay off its debt.

HEADING HOME

What should the country do with its former presidents? Maybe put them in the U.S. Senate. That was the idea behind several proposed amendments. Some folks didn't like the idea, though, since it would give the president's home state one more senator than the other states.

27

What the CONSTITUTION CREATED

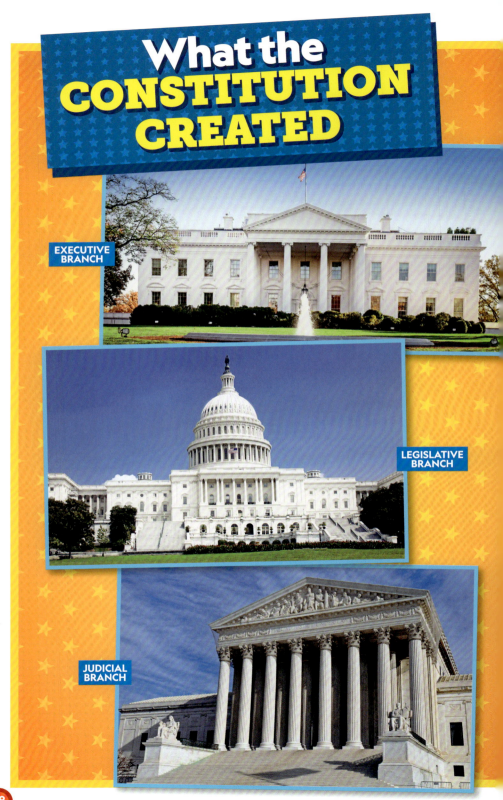

EXECUTIVE BRANCH

LEGISLATIVE BRANCH

JUDICIAL BRANCH

What does the federal government look like today? As the Founders wanted, Congress has two chambers, which are called the House of Representatives and the Senate. The House is home to 435 representatives. Each state sends a number of representatives based on its population—every state has at least one, and the most populous states have more than 20. Each state also has two senators, for a total of 100. See page 30 to learn more about Congress.

The executive branch is led by the president. This branch also includes the vice president and the heads of different government agencies. Many of these people form what is called the president's Cabinet and act as presidential advisers. A deep dive into the presidency and the executive branch starts on page 50.

The top court in the country's judicial system is called the Supreme Court. Today, it has nine members, but the Constitution didn't set that number. Instead, it lets Congress decide how many justices to include—and they can still change the number. Lawmakers also created a number of other federal courts. Turn to page 74 to learn more about the federal court system.

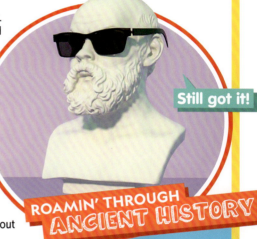

MEMBERS OF CONGRESS GET SOME SPECIAL BONUSES—LIKE GETTING TO PARK FOR FREE AT RONALD REAGAN NATIONAL AIRPORT IN WASHINGTON, D.C.

Still got it!

ROAMIN' THROUGH ANCIENT HISTORY

ROMAN ROOTS

Latin, the language of the Romans, has greatly influenced modern English, and that's true for politics and government, too. Here are some examples:

ENGLISH	LATIN
Capitol	*Capitolium*—the name of a temple for the main Roman god
Govern	*gubernare*—"to direct or steer"
Legislator	*legis lator*—"proposer of laws"
Republic	*res publica*—"public matter, or commonwealth"
Senate	*senex*—"old man"; originally the Roman Senate was made up of older men

The Founders knew their history and they paid close attention to the direct democracy created in Athens, Greece. But when writing the Constitution, they were more influenced by the republic in ancient Rome. Like Americans, the Romans had ditched their emperor and were looking for something different. In the government that formed over several centuries after that, wealthy Roman citizens shared power with the common people, called plebeians. The wealthy individuals, called patricians, served in the Senate, while the average Roman's views were represented in the assembly. Over time, the plebeians were also allowed to hold important government positions. This system was a model for the separation of powers and the checks and balances that Americans embraced.

CONGRESS: Crafting the Laws

LAWMAKERS IN THE HOUSE CHAMBER AT THE U.S. CAPITOL BUILDING

Do you have time to take a survey?

It's often said that two heads are better than one, and the Founders thought that same idea could be applied to Congress. They created what's called a bicameral legislature. "Bicameral" means "two houses," and it so happens to be another word with roots in Rome. (It comes from the Latin words *bi*, meaning "two," and *camera*, meaning "chambers.") The rooms where representatives and senators meet are called chambers.

As you have learned by now, the two houses of Congress are the House of Representatives and the Senate. Let's take a deeper look at the House of Representatives.

WHO'S IN THE HOUSE?

House of Representatives members serve two-year terms, and each House seat is up for election after each term. The Founders reasoned that if their terms were shorter, representatives would have to pay close attention to what voters wanted if they wanted to get reelected.

BY THE NUMBERS

States can gain or lose representatives as their population changes. After the 2020 Census, seven states lost one seat in the House, whereas six states gained at least one new seat.

THE U.S. CAPITOL BUILDING AT NIGHT

Because they represent fewer voters then senators, representatives are thought to have closer contact with their voters, also known as their constituents.

Today, each member of the House represents about 760,000 people in one region of a state, called a district. To determine the size of a district and how many representatives each state will have, every 10 years there is a census, or a counting of the U.S. population.

The House has special roles in the U.S. government, including the power to impeach, or bring legal charges against, the president or other government officials. Only the House can do this. You'll learn more about impeachment on page 62.

Members of the House serve on different committees that deal with topics such as energy, education, foreign affairs, the military, transportation, and the federal budget (how much money the government collects and how it spends that money). The committees decide which bills will go to the full House.

Most members of the House belong to political parties. The two major political parties in the United States are Democrats and Republicans. The party with the most members in the House gets to pick the chairs, or leaders, of the committees (see page 110 for more on political parties).

WHO CAN SERVE

According to the Constitution, a person who serves in the House must be
- ☐ at least 25 years old,
- ☐ a U.S. citizen for at least seven years, and
- ☐ a resident in the state they represent at the time of their election—but not necessarily a resident of their district.

If a representative dies or quits before the end of their term, the governor of their state calls a special election to choose a replacement.

YOU CAN SPOT MEMBERS OF THE HOUSE IN A CROWD BY THE SPECIAL PIN THEY WEAR. SOME LAWMAKERS WEAR THEIRS ON A NECKLACE.

Head of THE HOUSE

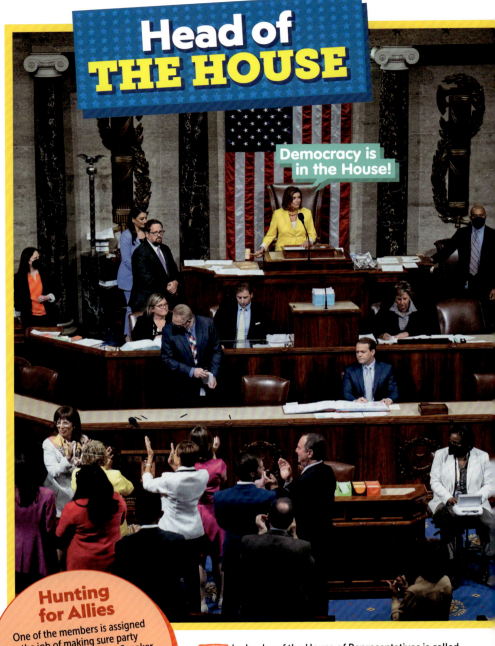

Democracy is in the House!

Hunting for Allies

One of the members is assigned the job of making sure party members vote the way the Speaker wants. They're called the whip. "Whip" comes from the expression "whipper-in," a person in fox hunting who makes sure the dogs don't stray during a chase.

The leader of the House of Representatives is called the Speaker of the House. The Constitution says the representatives must choose a Speaker. But the Founders didn't say a word about *how* members should choose a Speaker, or what the Speaker even does! Most experts agree that the Speaker doesn't *have* to be a member of the House, but so far, every Speaker has been an elected House representative.

PARTY POWER

Over time, the House itself has created rules and traditions that describe how the Speaker is chosen: The two major U.S. political parties in the House, the Republicans and the Democrats, choose one of their members to run for Speaker. Then, all the representatives vote for one of the two to be Speaker. Members almost always vote for their party's choice, so the Speaker is typically from the party with a majority—the most House representatives. With one of its members in charge, the majority party can control the process for writing bills.

THE SPEAKER'S SPECIAL

As the leader of the House, the Speaker does more than just speak. Their duties include the following:

- ★ Calling a session to order, which means getting the ball rolling when members meet.
- ★ Choosing the members of some committees.
- ★ Deciding which bills will be sent to which committees before the entire House considers them.
- ★ Calling on members to speak during debates.
- ★ Keeping order during debates!
- ★ Applying the rules of the House.
- ★ Acting as leader of their party in the House.
- ★ Last, but certainly not least, becoming the president if something happens to the president and vice president.

MADAM SPEAKER

In 2007, Nancy Pelosi became the 52nd Speaker of the House—and the first woman to hold this important position. A Democrat, she represented a district in San Francisco, California. You could say government service is in Pelosi's blood: Her father also served in Congress and was elected mayor of Baltimore. Years later, her brother also became Baltimore's mayor.

FIGHTING IS NOT ALLOWED DURING HOUSE DEBATES, BUT THAT HASN'T STOPPED SOME RAUCOUS REPS. IN 1858, ABOUT 30 MEMBERS FOUGHT ON THE HOUSE FLOOR OVER A BILL ABOUT SLAVERY. ONE MEMBER HAD HIS WIG RIPPED OFF HIS HEAD!

REALLY REMARKABLE REPS

While the Speaker is the head of the House, other members have also made their mark on U.S. history. Here's just a handful of those representatives, with the years they served in the House.

SHIRLEY CHISHOLM
(NEW YORK, 1969–1983)

The daughter of immigrants from Barbados and Guyana, Shirley Chisholm made history twice. She was the first Black woman elected to Congress, and the first woman to seek the presidency as a member of one of the country's two major parties. In 1972, she ran to become the Democratic Party's candidate for president. Fighting Shirley, as she was called, knew the odds of her winning were slim. But Chisholm wanted to draw attention to issues she cared deeply about, including ending the war the United States was fighting in Vietnam, giving more aid to the poor, and supporting the equal rights amendment for women.

JOHN QUINCY ADAMS
(MASSACHUSETTS, 1831–1848)

Sixth president of the United States, John Quincy Adams—along with his father John Adams—was part of the first father-son duo to serve as U.S. presidents. He went from the White House to the House and remains the only president to later serve in the House of Representatives. There, Adams spoke out strongly against slavery. He also fought for years against the House's so-called gag rule, which limited debate on slavery, until he won its repeal.

JAMES MADISON
(VIRGINIA, 1789–1797)

Remember him? He helped write the Constitution—in fact, he's known as the Father of the Constitution. As a member of the House, he proposed the amendments that make up the Bill of Rights. Madison later served in the Cabinet of President Thomas Jefferson and was elected president himself in 1808. At five feet four inches (1.6 m) tall, Madison was the shortest president ever, which earned him the nickname His Little Majesty.

GERALD FORD WAS THE **FOURTH** FORMER HOUSE MEMBER TO SERVE AS **PRESIDENT** WITHOUT BEING ELECTED, JOINING JOHN TYLER, MILLARD FILLMORE, AND ANDREW JOHNSON.

JEANNETTE RANKIN
(MONTANA, 1917–19, 1941–43)

In 1916, Jeannette Rankin was the first woman elected to Congress. By that time, women in her home state of Montana had had the right to vote for many years. In the House, she fought for voting rights for all American women, which finally came with the 19th Amendment, and she fought just as strongly against all wars. In 1917, she voted against the United States entering World War I (WWI) to fight Germany. Rankin was serving her second term in the House in 1941 when she voted not to declare war on Japan after it bombed U.S. ships in Pearl Harbor, Hawaii. She cast the sole vote against the declaration, making her the only representative to officially oppose the United States' entering both WWI and WWII.

Words of Wisdom
"I may be the first woman member of Congress, but I won't be the last."
—Jeannette Rankin

TAMMY DUCKWORTH
(ILLINOIS, 2013–17)

Tammy Duckworth can claim a lot of historic House "firsts." Born in Thailand, she was the first Thai American woman elected to Congress. She was also the first disabled woman to serve in Congress. In 2004, while serving as a helicopter pilot for U.S. forces fighting in Iraq, Duckworth was shot down, and she lost both her legs and partial use of her right arm. But that didn't stop her from winning election to the House, and then to the Senate. She scored another first as a senator—in 2018, she was the first woman to give birth while serving in the Senate. In the House, Duckworth worked to pass laws that help American military veterans.

CLOSE-UP: HOW MANY REPRESENTATIVES?

Distinct District

The typical district that a House representative serves has about 760,000 people. But several states, including Rhode Island and Wyoming, have populations smaller than the typical district.

The House of Representatives has grown over the years. The first Congress, which started in 1789, included 65 House members. As new states joined the Union, the House kept filling up with reps—until 1929, when a law set the number of representatives to 435. No new House seats have been added since.

MAP KEY

VIRGINIA ← State or territory
11
↑
Number of members in the U.S. House of Representatives

Delegates and the resident commissioner are nonvoting members of the U.S. House of Representatives.

DRAWING THE LINES

The population goes up and down from one census to the next. Rather than leave the boundaries of a congressional district the same size and shape on a map, lawmakers often make the area larger or smaller so that the district still has the same number of people. In most states, this process of redistricting is done by state lawmakers.

Since one political party usually has a majority in the state legislature, that party can shape the congressional districts to benefit itself. For example, a new district might be drawn to include more Republican than Democratic voters, or the other way around. Trying to add more voters of a certain party to a district is called gerrymandering. In some cases, state courts and the U.S. Supreme Court have found that gerrymandering illegally favors one party over the other. When this happens, lawmakers have to go back to the drawing board and create new districts. Gerrymandering is also an issue when lawmakers redraw district lines for state legislatures. As in the House, state lawmakers want to create new districts that favor their own party. That can lead to legal battles with members of the other party.

MORE SEATS!

Gerrymandering is a hotly debated issue in the House of Representatives. Another big concern is that the districts are too large. There's just too much work for one representative and their staff to do—they have to take care of the interests of almost 800,000 people after all! Some people have called for adding as many as 150 new seats in the House.

I don't see the resemblance ...

PUTTING THE GERRY IN GERRYMANDER

"Gerrymander" is sort of an odd word. It combines the word "salamander" with the name of Elbridge Gerry, one of the country's Founders. Gerry was governor of Massachusetts in 1812 when he signed a law that created an oddly shaped district for the state's senate. On a map, the district looked to some people—with vivid imaginations—like a salamander. So, "salamander" plus Gerry equals "gerrymander." The redistricting helped his political party win seats in the senate, and Gerry's name lives on to describe a process many Americans dislike.

37

House HISTORY

Here are some historical snapshots showing a few important firsts for the House of Representatives.

★ **First House of Representatives session: March 4, 1789**

The House met in New York City (Washington, D.C., didn't exist then!), but not enough members showed up for the House to do any business.

★ **First Black representative:**

Joseph Rainey of South Carolina, elected in 1870

★ **First Hispanic representative:**

Romualdo Pacheco of California, elected in 1876

★ **First Native American representative:**

Richard Cain of South Carolina, elected in 1872. His mother was Cherokee and his father was Black.

★ **First Japanese American representative:**

Daniel Inouye of Hawaii, elected in 1959

★ **First annual baseball game between members of the House and Senate:**

1909, organized by Representative John Tener of Pennsylvania

★ **First (and only) pair of sisters to serve in the House—at the same time!**

Linda Sanchez and Loretta Sanchez of California, who served together from 2003 to 2017

★ **First live radio broadcast of a debate in the House:**

December 19, 1922

38

AWW, MOM!

During the 1950s, Oliver Bolton and his mother, Frances, made history—they were the only mother and son to serve in the House at the same time. Both Boltons represented districts in Ohio. Frances won her first of 15 terms in 1938. Oliver was elected in 1952.

WHEN MEMBERS BREAK THE RULES

The Constitution lets the House and Senate punish members for "disorderly behavior" or breaking House rules. The House can even expel someone, or kick them out, if two-thirds of the members agree. To this day, only five members have faced this punishment. The first three were representatives who fought for the South during the Civil War. The other two were convicted of different crimes, including bribery. Members can also be punished with a censure, which is sort of like a public scolding in front of the whole House. The lightest punishment is a reprimand, or a censure that isn't done in public.

A Soup-er Lunch

One menu item in the House cafeteria always stays the same. A certain bean soup has been served every day since 1904, when it was the favorite soup of Joe Cannon, the House Speaker at that time. (If you're in the Senate and want bean soup, too, fear not! A similar soup is also served up each day in the Senate cafeteria.)

PICKING THE PRESIDENT

Choosing a U.S. president isn't always simple, as you'll see later on (page 118). The 12th Amendment says that if no candidate receives a clear majority of the votes, then the House of Representatives picks the prez! In the history of the United States, that's only happened three times. In 1801 and 1825, there was no clear winner in the electoral college, so House members chose Thomas Jefferson (1801) and John Quincy Adams (1825) as the new presidents. In 1877, Republicans challenged some of the electoral college votes in three states, saying they were cast illegally. The power to choose the president went to a special committee composed of representatives, senators, and Supreme Court justices, who then elected Rutherford B. Hayes.

Come and get it!

A HOUSE IN ORDER

To help keep order in the House, in 1789, the first representatives voted to create a job called the sergeant at arms. There have been 38 sergeants at arms in House history, and each served as the chief law enforcement officer in the House of Representatives. Today, the sarge, along with the Capitol Police, keeps House members safe in their part of the U.S. Capitol.

BY THE NUMBERS

Since 1789, more than 11,000 people have served in the House of Representatives. And 680 of those representatives have also served in the Senate.

GREAT DEBATE: HOW LONG SHOULD MEMBERS SERVE?

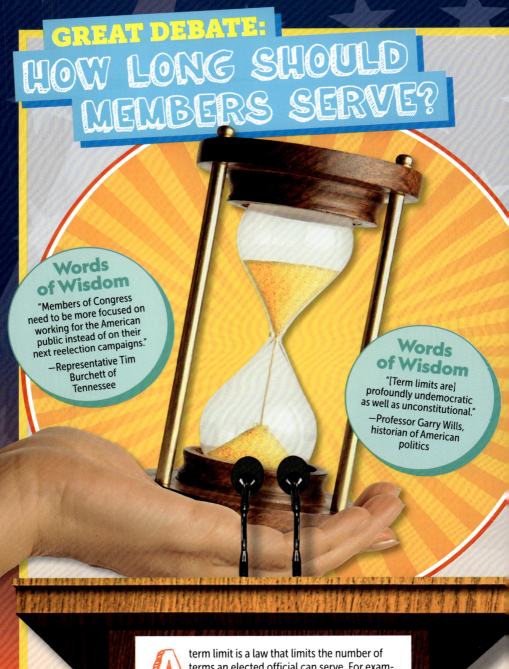

Words of Wisdom

"Members of Congress need to be more focused on working for the American public instead of on their next reelection campaigns."
—Representative Tim Burchett of Tennessee

Words of Wisdom

"[Term limits are] profoundly undemocratic as well as unconstitutional."
—Professor Garry Wills, historian of American politics

A term limit is a law that limits the number of terms an elected official can serve. For example, the president can serve only two four-year terms. But term limits don't exist for every office, including the House of Representatives, and not everyone likes the fact that members of Congress can serve for so long. Some Americans want to set term limits on representatives and senators, too. Here's a look at today's debate over term limits.

TERM LIMITS: YEA!

Here are a few popular arguments for why representatives should serve only a limited number of terms.

A person who currently holds a seat in Congress and who chooses to run for reelection is called an incumbent. About 90 percent of incumbents are reelected, and supporters of term limits often say it's too hard for a newcomer to challenge and defeat one. Incumbents already have strong relationships with donors, and the lawmakers rely on the money the donors give to help them win elections. People who favor limits say that those lawmakers care more about keeping their donors happy than their voters.

Placing term limits on Congress would create more open seats, with fewer incumbents running. Those running for an open seat would be on an even playing field—in theory, they wouldn't have the benefit of their long-standing political connections to help them raise money. Term limits would also give more people a chance to shape the country's laws.

Today, the influence a representative or senator has on Congress is based partly on seniority, or how long they've held their seat. Term limits would give more fresh-faced lawmakers a chance to fill the top positions that are usually held by those with higher seniority.

TERM LIMITS: NAY!

The Founders could have included term limits for Congress when writing the Constitution. Not only did some states at the time have limits, the Articles of Confederation included them, too. But in the end, the Founders decided to overlook matters regarding term limits in the Constitution for a couple of reasons.

Many of the Founders believed that voters should be able to choose the person they think will best represent them. And that person just might happen to be someone who has served a long time. Term limits would prevent voters from reelecting a well-liked incumbent. At least one Founder, Roger Sherman of Connecticut, also thought that shuffling members in and out of Congress would create an unstable government. The Founders liked stability.

Term limits would also kick out the most experienced members of Congress, and experience is important in running a government. Some people argue that if representatives only serve limited terms, they won't have the time to gain that experience—or they might not even bother to try.

BY THE NUMBERS

As of 2022, 15 states had term limits for their legislators, and 36 states had some sort of term limits for their governor.

IN HOUSE HISTORY, **JOHN DINGELL, JR.,** OF MICHIGAN HOLDS THE RECORD FOR **LONGEST SERVING REPRESENTATIVE.** HE SAT **IN OFFICE** FOR **59 YEARS!**

Not so fast, states!

THE CALL FOR AN AMENDMENT

A U.S. Supreme Court decision in 1995 said that states can't act on their own to limit terms for their members of Congress. The only way Americans can set congressional term limits is with an amendment to the Constitution. Since 1995, several lawmakers have introduced amendments to set term limits, but none of them have won enough support to go to the states for a vote. Such an amendment was introduced in both the House and Senate in 2021. It called for a three-term limit for representatives and a two-term limit for senators.

Making Sense of THE SENATE

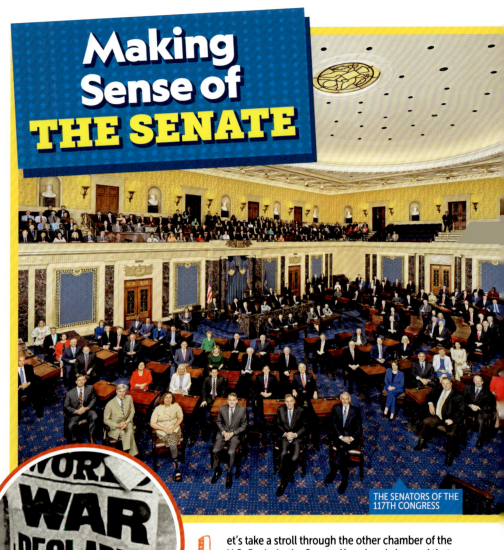

THE SENATORS OF THE 117TH CONGRESS

This Means War
The Senate shares one important power with the House. The two chambers together have the sole power to declare war. Since 1789, they have officially declared war 11 times.

Let's take a stroll through the other chamber of the U.S. Capitol—the Senate. You already learned that the Founders borrowed the idea of the Senate from ancient Rome, and that most states in 1787 had their own senates. Unlike the Roman senate, however, the U.S. Senate was not limited to wealthy citizens.

The Founders wanted senators to be older—and hopefully wiser—than representatives in the House. They also thought that state lawmakers would make better decisions than the average voter regarding who should represent their state in the Senate, an especially important choice since senators serve six-year terms, four years longer than House representatives. So, originally, the Constitution didn't allow voters to elect their senators. But that all changed when the 17th Amendment was passed, and now voters choose their state's senators.

WHAT SENATORS DO

The Senate, along with the House, proposes and passes bills. The Senate also has some powers all its own, such as

- ★ approving a president's choice of federal judges, ambassadors, and the heads of certain government agencies;
- ★ serving as a court after the House has impeached a government official; and
- ★ approving treaties with foreign governments.

Like the House, the Senate can punish its members, including booting them from the Senate. And, as in the House, senators serve on different committees that decide which bills will go to the full Senate. The political party with the most members in the Senate gets to pick the chairs, or leaders, of the committees.

LEADING THE WAY

The Senate doesn't have a powerful Speaker, like the House does. But it does have a majority leader from the party with the most senators. Like the Speaker, the majority leader chooses which bills the Senate will consider. The minority party also has a leader, and both parties have whips as well.

The Senate has its own president, a job that the Constitution says goes to the vice president. But it's not as impressive as it might sound—the vice president has only a few jobs: They preside, or watch over, the Senate's debates and votes. They vote only when it's to break a tie. And oddly enough, they can't even speak unless the senators agree to let them! As president of the Senate, the vice president also oversees the counting of electoral votes after a presidential election.

WHO CAN SERVE

According to the Constitution, senators must be

- ☐ at least 30 years old,
- ☐ a U.S. citizen for at least nine years, and
- ☐ a resident in the state they represent at the time of their election.

If a senator dies or quits before the end of their term, in most states the governor names a replacement who serves until the next regular election for that Senate seat. Thirteen states require a special election to fill the empty seat.

SUBSTITUTE VEEP

The Constitution also created one more leadership position in the Senate: the president pro tempore. *Pro tempore* is Latin, meaning "for the time being." The president pro tempore is elected by the Senate, is usually from the majority party, and fills in for the vice president when they're away. The temporary VP helps appoint people to some commissions and various other jobs. But the one thing they can't do is break a tie vote.

VICE PRESIDENT KAMALA HARRIS

SOME STANDOUT SENATORS

About 2,000 Americans have served in the U.S. Senate. Here's a look at just a few who made their mark on the country's history.

I've got the gift of gab.

DANIEL WEBSTER
(MASSACHUSETTS, 1827–1841, 1845–1850)

If there ever was a person who could talk up a storm, it was Daniel Webster. His speeches in the Senate led many to consider him one of the greatest orators, or public speakers, in U.S. history. Webster used his smarts and gift of gab to call for a strong national government. As slavery threatened to tear the country apart, he tried to keep the North and South united. In the end, that effort failed, leading to the Civil War. Webster never won the presidency—his dream job—but he did help guide the country's foreign affairs when he served as secretary of state. (Learn more about that job on page 68.)

Words of Wisdom
"Liberty and Union, now and forever, one and inseparable!"
—Daniel Webster

IN 1968, SENATOR **GEORGE MURPHY** STARTED A SWEET TRADITION: KEEPING CANDY AT HIS DESK. AFTER MURPHY, WHOEVER SITS AT THE "CANDY DESK" IS EXPECTED TO KEEP IT LOADED WITH SWEETS.

HIRAM REVELS
(MISSISSIPPI, 1870–71)

Hiram Revels made history as the first Black person to serve in Congress. In his home state of North Carolina, teaching Black children was against the law, but he still managed to start his education there before completing it in the North. In 1870, lawmakers in Mississippi chose him to fill one of the state's empty Senate seats until the end of the term the following year. Black people from many states asked for help from Revels, who saw himself as a defender of the rights of all African Americans.

NANCY KASSEBAUM
(KANSAS, 1978–1997)

It hasn't been easy for women to blaze their own trail. In 1978, Nancy Kassebaum became the first woman not following in her husband's footsteps to be elected to the Senate for a full six-year term. At the time, she was the only woman serving in the Senate. She was known to challenge presidents from her own Republican Party and won praise for her work on the Senate Committee on Foreign Relations. She also reached out to Democrats to work on issues like health care and the budget.

HATTIE CARAWAY
(ARKANSAS, 1931–1945)

After her husband died in 1931, Hattie Caraway was picked to fill his seat in the U.S. Senate, representing Arkansas. The next year, Caraway won a special election to complete the rest of her husband's term, becoming the first woman elected to the Senate. She went on to win reelection twice more. Caraway was a Democrat, and she was particularly interested in helping farmers suffering from the Great Depression, a period in which millions of Americans lost their jobs and struggled to get by.

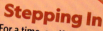

Stepping In
For a time, a wife of a U.S. lawmaker was sometimes chosen to fill her husband's seat if he died in office, as happened with Hattie Caraway. She was the first woman to enter the Senate that way.

THE FAMOUS FIVE

In 1955, the Senate created a committee to choose the greatest senators of all time. The head of the committee became pretty famous, too—it was John F. Kennedy, who later became the 35th president of the United States. Kennedy and his committee looked for senators who tried to help the country as a whole and worked with members from the other party, among other qualities. The committee chose five senators now known as the Famous Five: Daniel Webster of New Hampshire and Massachusetts (he served in Congress at different times for two different states!), Henry Clay of Kentucky, John C. Calhoun of South Carolina, Robert La Follette, Sr., of Wisconsin, and Robert Taft of Ohio. In 2004, the Senate added two more people to its informal hall of fame—Arthur Vandenberg of Michigan and Robert Wagner of New York.

SENATE MOMENTS

Throughout Senate history, certain senators have been the "first" to hold that office in some way. Here's a look at a few senators who changed the game.

FIRST HISPANIC SENATOR

Octaviano A. Larrazolo of New Mexico, elected in 1928

FIRST ASIAN AMERICAN SENATOR

Hiram Fong of Hawaii, elected in 1959

Wheeee!

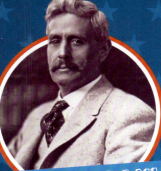

SENATORS HAVE HELD A **VARIETY OF JOBS** BEFORE WINNING THEIR SEAT. SOME HAVE EVEN **SHOT INTO SPACE!** JOHN GLENN, MARK KELLY, AND HARRISON SCHMITT WERE ALL **ASTRONAUTS** BEFORE SERVING IN THE **SENATE**.

FIRST NATIVE AMERICAN SENATORS

Robert L. Owen of Oklahoma and Charles Curtis of Kansas, both elected in 1907

46

FIRST BLIND SENATOR

Thomas P. Gore of Oklahoma, elected in 1907. He lost his sight as a child.

FROM THE SENATE TO THE WHITE HOUSE

If you want a head start on running for president, it just might help to be a senator first. Out of the 45 people who've been elected president, almost 40 percent served in the Senate first. James Monroe, the fifth president, was the first to go from the Senate chamber to the White House. In the 21st century, two presidents have made that leap: Barack Obama and Joe Biden. Others in the senator-to-president club include Richard Nixon, John F. Kennedy, Harry Truman, and Andrew Jackson.

FIRST SENATOR TO HAVE WON AN OLYMPIC GOLD MEDAL

Bill Bradley of New Jersey, elected in 1979. He played for the 1964 U.S. basketball team.

FIRST SPOUSE OF A PRESIDENT TO BECOME A SENATOR

Hillary Clinton of New York, elected in 2000

BY THE NUMBERS

The U.S. Senate has had 73 members who were born outside the country. The top three countries of origin for those senators are

★ Ireland with 16 senators,
★ Canada with 13 senators, and
★ England with 13 senators.

Other countries that senators have come from include Cuba, Japan, and Mexico.

GREAT DEBATE: BUST THE FILIBUSTER

I'm timing you!

What's one way to slow down the lawmaking process in the Senate? Start a filibuster. With this action, senators can delay a vote on bills they don't like. In the past, senators talked, and talked, and talked during a filibuster, sometimes for hours at a time. This delaying tactic only happens in the Senate, and the rules for a filibuster have changed over the years. It used to be that a senator had to talk nonstop to keep a filibuster going. By the early 1900s, a filibuster would end if two-thirds of the Senate voted to end it—a process called cloture.

Today, senators don't have to actually speak to start a filibuster. All they have to do is say they don't like a bill, and unless the majority party can secure 60 votes to end the tedious talk before it starts, the bill won't be debated at all. Because cloture requires 60 votes, unless one party has a huge majority in the Senate, it's hard to achieve.

Today's filibuster rules have led some lawmakers to call for changing it—or getting rid of the filibuster altogether. Here are the arguments for and against the filibuster.

KEEP THE FILIBUSTER

Supporters of the filibuster say it helps protect the minority party, especially if one party has only a small majority. The minority party can filibuster bills that it believes are harmful but that the other party could otherwise easily push through the Senate with just 51 votes.

Another related benefit: The filibuster forces the majority party to make compromises if it wants to pass a bill. Compromise can lead to bills that benefit a wider variety of Americans rather than the supporters of just one party or the other.

Some senators want to keep the filibuster but make it harder to use. One idea is to go back to making senators talk endlessly on the Senate floor to keep a filibuster alive. Another idea is to lower the number of votes needed for cloture.

CAN THE FILIBUSTER

Some don't like the idea that the minority party, or even one senator, can stop the process of debating a bill—especially if it's a bill most people favor. And where people live is shaping how much power states have in the Senate. More Americans are living in states with large populations, but since each state has the same number of senators, those Americans are represented by fewer senators. The filibuster gives one senator from a state with a tiny population the power to stop what most Americans may want.

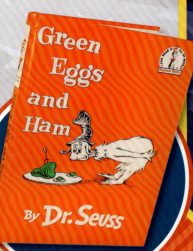

Words of Wisdom
"The Senate is where people who live in low-population states have a voice. The filibuster makes this possible."
—Senator Mike Enzi of Wyoming

TO TAKE UP TIME, SENATORS CAN TALK ABOUT WHATEVER THEY WANT. DURING FILIBUSTERS, SENATORS HAVE **READ SHAKESPEARE,** A RECIPE FOR FRIED OYSTERS, AND EVEN **GREEN EGGS AND HAM,** BY DR. SEUSS!

Words of Wisdom
"The filibuster is an effort to talk something to death."
—Senator Dick Durbin of Illinois

BY THE NUMBERS
Strom Thurmond of South Carolina could talk up a storm. In 1957, he set a filibuster record when he spoke for 24 hours and 18 minutes!

The EXECUTIVE BRANCH

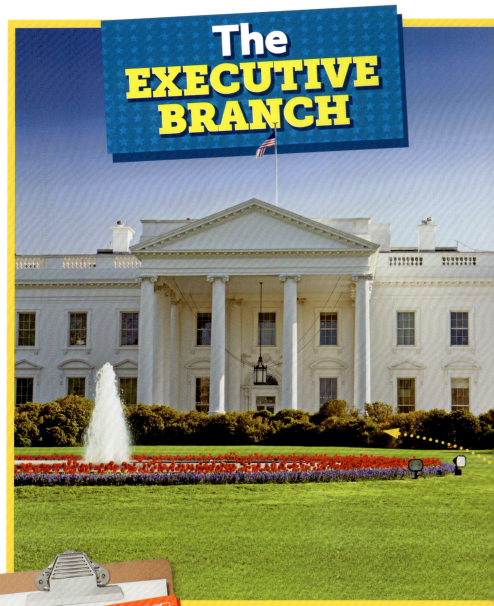

WHO CAN SERVE

According to the Constitution, the president must
- be at least 35 years old,
- be a natural-born citizen—meaning they were born in U.S. territory or abroad to U.S. citizens, and
- have lived in the country for a minimum of 14 years.

You've seen what Congress, as the legislative branch, does. Let's move to another branch in the government "tree." The executive branch executes, or carries out, laws passed by Congress and approved by the president, who leads the branch.

Helping the president are the vice president and the heads of the different agencies within the executive branch. You'll learn more about these folks in a bit. Let's focus first on the leader of the country, the prez.

50

HAIL TO THE CHIEF!

Being president is no easy job. Along with approving or rejecting laws passed by Congress, the presidential duties (some of which are listed in the Constitution—others, "informal powers," developed over time) include these:

★ Serves as head of the government and head of state. This means the president is the main representative of the U.S. government when dealing with other nations.

★ Acts as commander in chief of the military, to defend the country and its interests.

★ Chooses the heads of executive branch departments, agencies such as the Central Intelligence Agency (CIA), and ambassadors who represent the United States overseas.

★ Chooses federal judges and appoints new justices to the Supreme Court.

★ Issues executive orders, statements the president signs to direct how laws are carried out by other members of the executive branch.

★ Signs treaties, or negotiated agreements between countries.

★ Pardons, or excuses, people who break federal laws.

★ Serves as leader of their political party.

★ Uses the power of the presidency to gain support for their policies and decisions.

★ Issues "signing statements," which reflect their views on certain parts of a bill they have signed into law.

PRESIDENTIAL PERKS

The job sure is tough, but every president gets some perks, or benefits, that make their life a little easier. For example, they get a paycheck of about $400,000 every year. That doesn't include the $50,000 they get for food and other personal needs, plus more for travel and entertainment. The president and their family also get to live in a pretty cool place—the White House! The president receives 24/7 protection by special agents, called the Secret Service. And the president has their own jumbo jet, called Air Force One. They even get their own song. "Hail to the Chief" is played anytime the president attends a formal event.

The perks don't stop when a president's term ends. They still earn more than $200,000 every year for life, and they keep their Secret Service protection!

I'm fancy.

JOHN ADAMS THOUGHT THE PRESIDENT SHOULD BE ADDRESSED AS "HIS HIGHNESS, THE PRESIDENT OF THE UNITED STATES, AND PROTECTOR OF THEIR LIBERTIES."

Precious cargo comin' through!

SOME PROMINENT PRESIDENTS

Triple-check me, pls!

Being the leader of a rich and powerful nation is a tall order, and some presidents have handled the responsibility better than others. According to one recent poll of U.S. historians, these five are often considered the cream of the presidential crop.

GEORGE WASHINGTON (1789-1797)

Being the first at something can be tricky, but George set an example that other presidents have tried to follow. After leading the new United States to victory in the American Revolution, Washington was just about everyone's pick to be the first prez—he is the only president to have been elected with every electoral vote! Despite his presidential popularity, Washington didn't want to seem like a king, since Americans had just gotten rid of one. So, he chose to wear everyday clothes rather than a special uniform. He also ran for only two terms, at a time when the Constitution didn't limit how long a president could serve.

George Washington was **WORRIED THAT HE MIGHT BE ACCIDENTALLY BURIED ALIVE,** so he insisted he not be buried until at least three days after he was thought dead.

ABRAHAM LINCOLN (1861-65)

Abe who?

Not everyone was happy when Abraham Lincoln was elected president. Seven states that allowed slavery soon voted to leave the Union because they feared Lincoln would end it. (Four more states joined them later.) In response, Lincoln said the states had no legal right to leave. The result: the Civil War in 1861–65. During the war, Lincoln issued the Emancipation Proclamation, which freed many enslaved Americans. But it wouldn't be until April 1865, when the North finally won the war, that freedom was granted to all enslaved people in the U.S.

Abraham Lincoln hated being called Abe so much, **EVEN HIS WIFE CALLED HIM MR. LINCOLN!**

52

On a hunt, Theodore Roosevelt **REFUSED TO KILL AN OLD BEAR** his guide had found. In honor of that, a shop owner **BEGAN SELLING SMALL STUFFED BEARS HE CALLED TEDDY BEARS** (though T.R. hated being called Teddy).

THEODORE ROOSEVELT (1901–09)

Theodore Roosevelt had many interests. He wrote books, owned a ranch, hunted in Africa, and organized a group of volunteer soldiers called the Rough Riders to fight in the war against Spain in 1898. In the White House, his accomplishments included authorizing the building of the Panama Canal, limiting the power of some big businesses, and creating five national parks to protect wildlife. Roosevelt was also the first president to fly in an airplane, dive in a submarine, visit a foreign country, win a Nobel Peace Prize, and invite an African American to dine at the White House.

FRANKLIN D. ROOSEVELT (1933–1945)

A distant cousin of Theodore, Franklin D. Roosevelt was elected president four times—a record that will never be broken as long as the 22nd Amendment remains in effect. FDR led the United States during some of its most difficult years. When he took office, the country was in the middle of the Great Depression, a period of terrible economic collapse. To end the Depression, he created the New Deal, which included important programs like Social Security, a form of insurance that pays people money after they retire and provides other monetary aid. After Japan bombed the U.S. Navy base at Pearl Harbor, Hawaii, in 1941, drawing the U.S. into the Second World War (WWII), Roosevelt led military forces across four continents as commander in chief.

DWIGHT D. EISENHOWER (1953–1961)

I like Ike!

Known as Ike, Dwight D. Eisenhower was one of the generals who helped the United States win WWII. After the war, Americans liked Ike so much that they elected him president. Soon after taking office, he helped end the Korean War (1950–53). Eisenhower had other big accomplishments: Ike's support of the interstate highway system was instrumental in getting it built. And, under his watch, the country launched its first satellites into space.

Students in Dwight Eisenhower's high school class **VOTED HIS BROTHER AS MOST LIKELY TO BECOME PRESIDENT.** They thought Ike would be a history teacher!

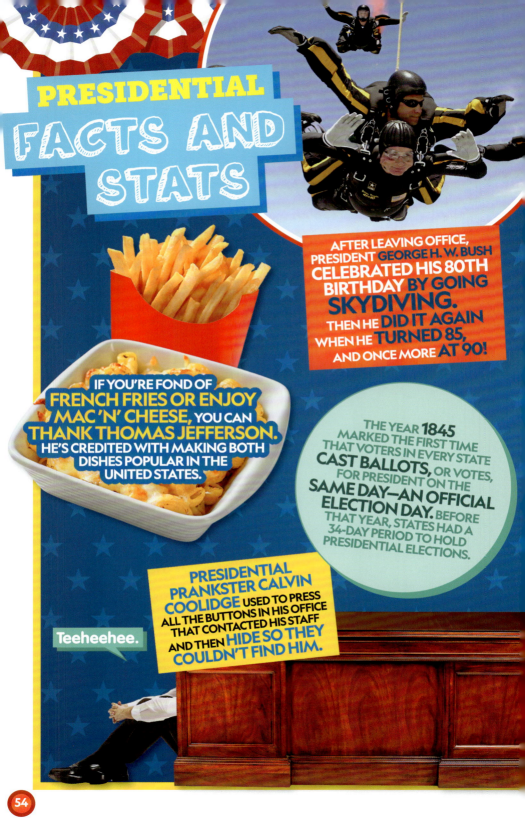

PRESIDENTIAL FACTS AND STATS

AFTER LEAVING OFFICE, PRESIDENT GEORGE H. W. BUSH CELEBRATED HIS 80TH BIRTHDAY BY GOING SKYDIVING. THEN HE DID IT AGAIN WHEN HE TURNED 85, AND ONCE MORE AT 90!

IF YOU'RE FOND OF FRENCH FRIES OR ENJOY MAC 'N' CHEESE, YOU CAN THANK THOMAS JEFFERSON. HE'S CREDITED WITH MAKING BOTH DISHES POPULAR IN THE UNITED STATES.

THE YEAR 1845 MARKED THE FIRST TIME THAT VOTERS IN EVERY STATE CAST BALLOTS, OR VOTES, FOR PRESIDENT ON THE SAME DAY—AN OFFICIAL ELECTION DAY. BEFORE THAT YEAR, STATES HAD A 34-DAY PERIOD TO HOLD PRESIDENTIAL ELECTIONS.

PRESIDENTIAL PRANKSTER CALVIN COOLIDGE USED TO PRESS ALL THE BUTTONS IN HIS OFFICE THAT CONTACTED HIS STAFF AND THEN HIDE SO THEY COULDN'T FIND HIM.

Teeheehee.

ONE **NICKNAME FOR THE PRESIDENT IS POTUS,** WHICH STANDS FOR "PRESIDENT OF THE UNITED STATES."

ZACHARY TAYLOR **NEVER VOTED BEFORE HE RAN** FOR PRESIDENT IN 1848.

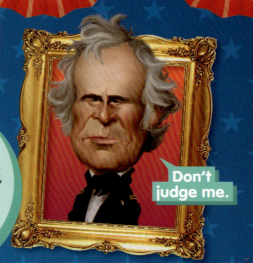

Don't judge me.

>> **WHEN IT COMES TO PRESIDENTIAL PETS, THEODORE ROOSEVELT WAS THE ZOOKEEPER IN CHIEF. ALONG WITH SEVERAL DOGS, THE ANIMALS HIS FAMILY KEPT AT THE WHITE HOUSE INCLUDED GUINEA PIGS, A LIZARD, A PONY, A RABBIT, A PIG, A BADGER, AND EVEN A SMALL BEAR!**

Hail to THE VEEP

Listen up!

Words of Wisdom

"I am vice president. In this I am nothing, but I may be everything."
—John Adams

The VP is the second highest office in the United States. One of the most important roles of the VP is to step in to fill the president's role during times of calamity, such as when a president is too sick or unable to do their job. Known as the "veep," several veeps have made the move to the White House after a president died, but it took the 25th Amendment to formally make this the law of the land. This amendment also says that if the vice president dies or chooses to leave office, the president has the power to name a new one, whom Congress must then approve.

A GROWING ROLE

In the country's early years, the position of vice president was filled by the presidential candidate who had the second highest number of electoral votes. The president and the vice president could be from different political parties. Now, the presidential candidate asks someone to run with them as the candidate for vice president, so the people running for the two top executive offices are always from the same party. The two candidates form what's called their party's ticket. The vice presidential candidate is referred to as the presidential candidate's running mate.

Outside their duties in the Senate, most early vice presidents didn't have much to do. Until the 1920s, vice presidents didn't even join the president's Cabinet of top advisers. But since the 1960s, most presidents have given their second-in-command larger roles in the executive branch. At home, the vice president leads special commissions and tries to convince Congress to pass laws that the president supports. Abroad, in foreign countries, vice presidents represent the U.S. government.

Since 1796, starting with John Adams, six vice presidents were later elected president. And eight vice presidents have moved up in the executive branch after a president died in office. The first was John Tyler in 1841, who became president after the death of William Henry Harrison.

Guys, can't you talk it out?

BAD BURR

If you've seen *Hamilton*, the musical, you already know about one vice president: Aaron Burr. In 1804, while he was the vice president (Thomas Jefferson was the president), he took part in a famous duel during which he killed Alexander Hamilton, one of the Founders of the United States. He was charged with murder but did not face trial, thanks in part to help from senators who supported him. After a brief time in South Carolina, Burr returned to Washington, D.C., and finished his term. He got into more trouble a few years later when he was accused of treason. Although Burr was found not guilty, many Americans considered him a traitor.

A VERY HISTORIC VEEP

In 2020, Kamala Harris made history when she was elected the 49th vice president—the first woman to hold this prestigious office. With a mother from India and a father from Jamaica, Harris was also the first person of color to become vice president. That's two important firsts! Harris began her political career in California, where she served as the state's attorney general—the government's top lawyer. In 2016, she was elected to the U.S. Senate, and in 2020, Harris entered the race to become the Democratic Party's candidate for president. However, the party ultimately chose Joe Biden, who then asked Harris to join his ticket as his vice presidential running mate.

Going to COLLEGE

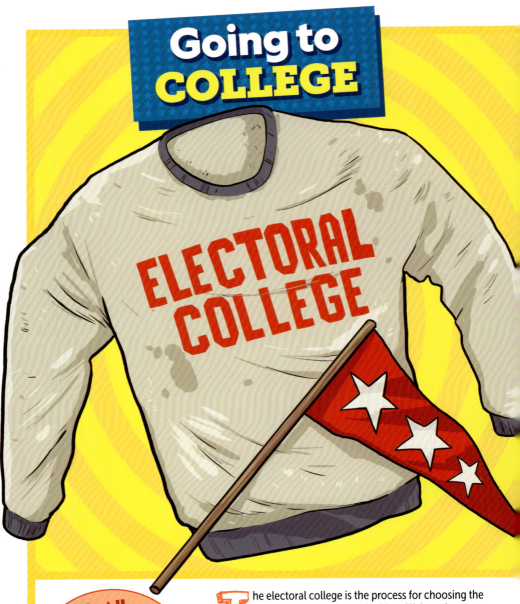

It All Adds Up

The number of electoral votes is equal to the number of senators and House representatives each state sends to Congress, plus three votes for the District of Columbia, for a total of 538.

The electoral college is the process for choosing the president. You might be thinking, *Wait a minute, don't voters pick the president and vice president?* And you'd be right—sort of.

Before an election, each political party chooses electors, people who they feel will support the party's chosen candidate. During the election, voters cast ballots for one candidate or another. Then, each state's electors cast their votes. Electors are expected to vote for their party's candidate if they won their state, but the Constitution doesn't actually require it. To become president, candidates need 270 electoral votes—just over half of the electoral college.

WINNING LOSERS

The candidate who wins the popular vote, or the votes cast by regular voters, doesn't automatically become president, though they usually do. Five times so far, a candidate has won the popular vote but has not received enough electoral votes to win the presidency:

YEAR	ELECTED PRESIDENT	WINNER OF POPULAR VOTE
1824	John Quincy Adams	Andrew Jackson
1876	Rutherford B. Hayes	Samuel Tilden
1888	Benjamin Harrison	Grover Cleveland
2000	George W. Bush	Al Gore
2016	Donald Trump	Hillary Clinton

ELECTORAL EVENTS CLOSE-UP

The Constitution says electors can't be members of Congress or hold office in the federal government. States get to decide how to choose electors, and major parties usually choose them during state conventions before the November election.

In every state but two, the winning candidate receives all the states' electoral votes—a true winner-takes-all scenario. Maine and Nebraska are a little different. They allow one vote for each of their districts, with the rest going to the candidate who won the popular vote. This means that, depending on who wins the popular vote in each district, both candidates from the major parties could win electoral votes in the same state.

In December, the electors of each state meet to cast their votes. These ballots are sent to Congress, and they're officially counted on January 6. Members of Congress can object to the votes if they think something suspicious happened during the election, but the electoral votes are usually accepted. The vice president, acting as president of the Senate, then announces, "We have a winner!"

COUNTING ON CONGRESS

The electoral college process has had some hiccups over the years. Three times, Congress had to step in and declare the winner:

★ **1801:** Both Thomas Jefferson and Aaron Burr received 73 electoral votes, so the House had to choose the president. It went with Jefferson.

★ **1825:** Neither Andrew Jackson nor John Quincy Adams won a majority of the electoral votes. Once again, the House had to decide. It chose Adams.

★ **1877:** Republicans in Congress challenged the electoral votes from three states. Congress then set up a special commission to decide the winner—Rutherford B. Hayes.

i can Hayes presidency?

AN ELECTOR WHO DOESN'T VOTE FOR THE CANDIDATE WHO WON IN THEIR STATE IS CALLED A FAITHLESS ELECTOR.

GREAT DEBATE: DO WE NEED THE ELECTORAL COLLEGE?

The Founders rejected the idea of simply going with the country's popular vote or having Congress pick the president. Instead, they saw the electoral college as a way to give the states some say in choosing the commander in chief. Over time, though, some people started to feel the electoral college process was flawed. Americans have considered changing the electoral college, or even getting rid of it. The call for change often comes after a president loses the popular vote but wins in the electoral college, like with George W. Bush and Al Gore in 2000 or Donald Trump and Hillary Clinton in 2016. But some folks think things should stay as they are. Let's take a deeper look at the pros and cons of the electoral college.

KEEP THE COLLEGE

Some political experts argue that the electoral college is a good thing. It forces candidates to try to win support from a diverse group of people all across the country. The candidates need as many electoral votes as possible, so they can't focus only on states or regions with a large number of voters. The college, supporters say, gives smaller states and rural regions an important role in choosing the president.

Some supporters say the electoral college is also useful when there are more than two candidates running. If the president were picked just by popular vote, then there could be instances in which none of the candidates won a majority of the votes. This would force a second election, called a runoff. The Constitution doesn't have a system for addressing runoffs, but it does have rules in place for choosing a president if no candidate receives enough electoral votes to win.

Words of Wisdom
"The current electoral college system creates a needed balance between rural and urban interests."
—State legislature of South Dakota

CAN THE COLLEGE

Opponents of the electoral college argue that the current system forces candidates to spend a lot of time seeking votes in certain states called swing states, whose electoral votes can swing the election from one candidate to the other. This is because swing states tend to have a fairly equal number of voters from each major party. At the same time, candidates spend *less* time in states that have solid Democratic or Republican majorities, since it's easier to predict which way those states will go. Voters in these states sometimes end up feeling ignored.

Others think the college is just unfair. A majority of voters across the country might want one candidate, but the vote in the electoral college could give the presidency to someone else. That's because the college gives some states more influence than others in deciding the race.

Words of Wisdom
"You can't let 538 people decide the fate of a country of 300 million people."
—Former elector Robert Nemanich, from Colorado

A COLLEGE COMPROMISE?

Some people have said there's a way to keep the college *and* have the popular vote choose the president. With the National Popular Vote Interstate Compact, states pass laws that require their electoral voters to vote for the candidate who wins the popular vote. As of 2022, 15 states and the District of Columbia, with a total of 195 votes, have approved the compact, which would officially take effect if (or when) it has the support of 270 electoral votes.

BY THE NUMBERS

Members of Congress have proposed at least 700 amendments to change the electoral college or get rid of it altogether.

EX-EXECUTIVE

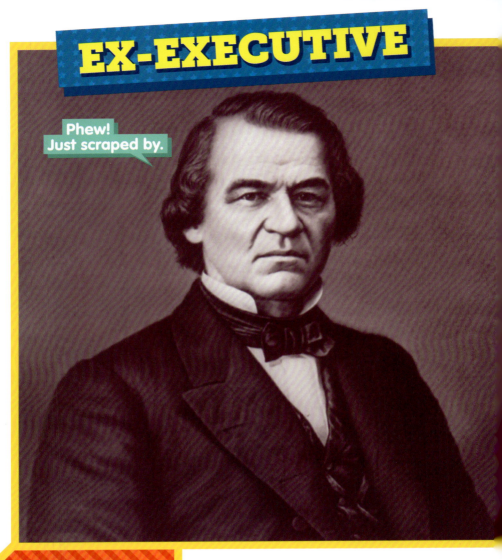

Phew! Just scraped by.

IN HIS TRIAL IN THE U.S. SENATE, ANDREW JOHNSON KEPT HIS JOB AS PRESIDENT BY JUST ONE VOTE ON THE LAST ARTICLE OF IMPEACHMENT.

So, you've learned how Americans choose their presidents. Now let's get into what they do if they want to get rid of one—if, for example, the president commits a crime or does something equally disagreeable. When this happens, Congress can begin what's called impeachment.

The process of impeachment usually starts in the House of Representatives in one of two ways:

1. One member makes a proposal, called a resolution, accusing the president of breaking the law or misusing their power.
2. The House Judiciary Committee investigates charges against the president and then recommends bringing impeachment charges to the whole House.

THE SENATE VOTES DURING AN IMPEACHMENT TRIAL OF PRESIDENT DONALD TRUMP.

Either way, the charges are called articles of impeachment, and the House can vote to accept or reject any of the articles, depending on the evidence presented.

A TRIAL IN THE SENATE

If the House approves one or more articles of impeachment, the case moves to the Senate. The Senate acts as a jury, or a group of people randomly chosen to decide whether someone is innocent. The Chief Justice of the United States presides over the trial, and several House members act as lawyers to present the facts against the president. The president has their own lawyers who argue for their innocence.

If two-thirds of the senators believe the president is guilty on even just one article of impeachment, the president is removed from office. And if they're guilty, the Senate can vote to prevent them from holding federal office again.

PAST PRESIDENTS IMPEACHED

Only three presidents have been impeached by the House: Andrew Johnson, Bill Clinton, and Donald Trump. The Senate didn't convict any of them, so they all continued to serve as president. One president, Richard Nixon, was on the verge of being impeached by the House in 1974, but he chose to resign before the House could vote. Donald Trump is the only president to have been impeached by the House twice—once in 2019 and again in 2021.

MORE PEOPLE IMPEACHED

Impeachment isn't just for presidents. Any federal official can be removed by this process. The only difference is that the Chief Justice presides in the Senate only when the president is on the stand. Ever since the first articles of impeachment were passed in the House in 1797, more judges have faced impeachment than any other government official. One senator and one Cabinet member have also been impeached. Out of 20 impeachment trials conducted in the Senate, senators have voted to remove only eight people, while three resigned before the process was completed.

New record!

A Set of SECRETARIES

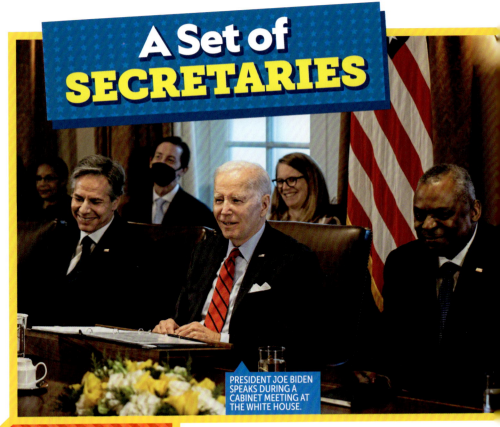

PRESIDENT JOE BIDEN SPEAKS DURING A CABINET MEETING AT THE WHITE HOUSE.

PRESIDENT JOHN F. KENNEDY MADE HIS BROTHER ROBERT THE ATTORNEY GENERAL. A 1967 LAW ENDED UP MAKING IT ILLEGAL FOR A PRESIDENT TO NAME A RELATIVE TO A CABINET POSITION.

Every president has a Cabinet, which is made up of the people who lead the different departments that are part of the executive branch. These include the Department of Transportation, the Department of Health and Human Services, and the Department of Agriculture. The department leaders are called secretaries—except for the attorney general, who heads the Department of Justice. Today's Cabinet also includes the vice president, and sometimes other government officials as well.

Cabinet members serve as top advisers to the president. They also carry out a president's orders within their departments. Executive department leaders must be approved by the Senate, but after that, only the president can fire them if they aren't up to the job.

AN EVER EXPANDING CABINET

Among his many firsts, George Washington held the very first Cabinet meeting in 1791. The executive branch had only three departments then—Treasury, State, and War—each represented by one Cabinet member. Congress also created the position of attorney general, which became the fourth Cabinet member. (The attorneys general didn't get to lead their own department until 1870.) Washington tried to pick Cabinet members with a wide range of experiences and personal backgrounds.

Over the years, the executive branch grew as Congress created new departments. Today, there are 15 departments, with the head of each serving in the Cabinet. Some presidents have included other officials in their Cabinet. For example, the U.S. ambassador to the United Nations was in the Cabinet of both Presidents Ronald Reagan and Joe Biden.

THE CABINET TODAY

The heads of the 15 executive departments are in the Cabinet. The departments are listed in order of when they were created. If the president, vice president, Speaker of the House, and Senate president pro tempore are all not available to serve as president, the list also shows the Cabinet member who is next in line, which is called the presidential succession.

1. State
2. Treasury
3. Defense
4. Attorney General
5. Interior
6. Agriculture
7. Commerce
8. Labor
9. Health and Human Services
10. Housing and Urban Development
11. Transportation
12. Energy
13. Education
14. Veterans Affairs
15. Homeland Security

COOKING SOMETHING UP

President Andrew Jackson had a problem: Some of his Cabinet members were not the best of buddies. To avoid potential problems, he decided to meet with several members, along with a few trusted friends, outside the formal Cabinet meetings. Some newspapers called this informal get-together Jackson's "Kitchen Cabinet," and they used the term as a criticism against Jackson. The unofficial Cabinet lasted only a few years. But the term lives on—it's used to describe any informal group of advisers to a government leader, particularly the president.

U.S. AMBASSADOR TO THE UNITED NATIONS LINDA THOMAS-GREENFIELD SPEAKS AT A MEETING OF THE UN SECURITY COUNCIL.

PRESIDENTIAL PARTNERS

There's one person in the White House who knows the president pretty well—their spouse. So far, all the presidential spouses have been women and they are known as the first lady, or FLOTUS for short (first lady of the United States). A male presidential spouse would be called the first gentleman.

The Constitution doesn't mention the president's partner, and neither do any laws passed by Congress. But throughout history, first ladies have held important roles and had their own staff of up to 25 people.

Here's a look at some of the first ladies in U.S. history.

MARTHA WASHINGTON (1789–1797)

The *first* first lady knew that how she performed would shape the role of future first ladies, though this title wasn't yet used in her time. Martha Washington had to run the new presidential home *and* oversee care of the Washingtons' home, Mount Vernon. She also had to entertain visitors who came to meet her husband.

SOME GUESTS CALLED MARTHA WASHINGTON "LADY WASHINGTON." OTHERS TRIED OUT "OUR LADY PRESIDENTRESS" FOR SIZE, BUT THAT ONE DIDN'T CATCH ON.

ELEANOR ROOSEVELT (1933–1945)

Eleanor Roosevelt served as a role model for future first ladies who wanted to play an active role in government. She was the *first* first lady to meet publicly with news reporters. Because she would only meet with women reporters, many newspapers had to hire their first women reporters to cover her press conferences. Roosevelt often traveled around the United States and reported back to her husband, President Franklin D. Roosevelt, what she learned from average Americans. She was also a strong supporter of equal rights for all Americans, at a time when the laws in some states made it hard for Black people to vote and kept them from using the same public spaces as white people.

Words of Wisdom

"You gain strength, courage and confidence by every experience in which you really stop to look fear in the face … You must do the thing you think you cannot do."

—Eleanor Roosevelt

66

NANCY REAGAN
(1981–89)

Like her husband, Ronald Reagan, Nancy Reagan acted in films before she took on her biggest role: serving as first lady. Before coming to Washington with her husband, Reagan was first lady of California. There, she often spent time visiting veterans and people with physical or mental disabilities. As FLOTUS, Reagan promoted programs that worked to end drug and alcohol abuse among young Americans, telling them to "just say no."

HILLARY RODHAM CLINTON
(1993–2001)

As first lady, Hillary Rodham Clinton tried to educate others about the problems women and children face in the United States and around the world. She promoted programs to give children vaccines to prevent them from getting certain illnesses. She also said women everywhere should always have the same rights as men. In 2001, Clinton made history when she became the first former first lady to become a U.S. senator. She later served as secretary of state under President Barack Obama. Clinton made history once more in 2016 when she became the Democratic presidential nominee, making her the first woman from one of the two major parties to hold that distinction.

Department DETAILS

The Department of the Treasury, the Department of State, the Department of Defense, and the Department of Justice are considered the biggies—their heads were the first four Cabinet members ever! Let's take a closer look.

DEPARTMENT OF THE TREASURY

Role: Keeping an eye on the government's piggy bank. The secretary of the treasury helps the president pursue policies that will create jobs and improve the economy. The treasury has different agencies, called bureaus, with lots of duties. One bureau is in charge of printing the country's paper money, another makes coins, and a completely different one collects federal taxes.

DEPARTMENT OF STATE

Role: Handles the country's relations with foreign nations. The department is in charge of embassies—the places where Americans can go for help—around the world. Embassies also serve as the home of some of the ambassadors who represent the U.S. government in those countries.

DEPARTMENT OF DEFENSE

Role: This department was originally called the Department of War. Today, it's the largest executive department, with more than 2.9 million members of the military and support staff. All the different branches of the military defend U.S. interests and help the country's allies around the world.

DEPARTMENT OF JUSTICE

Role: Break a federal law, and you might just have a member of the Justice Department looking for you or trying you in court. This department handles all the legal cases involving the federal government. The FBI, which is also a part of this department, tracks down all kinds of crooks, including terrorists. Another bureau focuses on people who smuggle (or illegally carry) drugs or weapons into or out of the country. The Justice Department has 93 attorneys who bring accused criminals to trial.

THE FBI HAS A FILE ON BIGFOOT!

You'll never catch me!

LAND, FOOD, AND MONEY

After the first four, these three departments were the ones created next, between 1849 and 1903:

DEPARTMENT OF THE INTERIOR

Role: Protects wildlife and manages the use of public lands. The department also helps educate Americans about these lands and their resources. Interior officials handle issues related to the country's Native American people. And when an earthquake hits, one of its bureaus measures how strong it was.

A BIG Job
The department oversees 420 million acres of federal land— an area about the size of Alaska.

DEPARTMENT OF AGRICULTURE

Role: Helps American farmers produce a lot of food, which we all need! It also helps Americans choose healthy food, improves their access to it, and works to make sure that food is safe to eat. Like the Interior, the Department of Agriculture helps protect some lands and restore those that have been damaged.

Lunch Is Served!
The department's school lunch program provides free or low-cost meals to more than 30 million kids every school day.

DEPARTMENT OF COMMERCE

Role: Helps companies buy and sell goods, both within the United States and overseas. The department is also home to the Census Bureau, which counts the American population every 10 years and is the source for all sorts of stats. And when you're wondering if you'll see sun or snow, the department's National Weather Service can let you know!

69

Department DETAILS continued

NEXT UP
These departments are all about work, housing, and getting around.

DEPARTMENT OF TRANSPORTATION

Role: If you've ever ridden in a car, a train, or a plane, you've experienced some of this department's work. It has specific agencies, called administrations, to make sure highways, railways, and airplanes are safe. One of them, the National Highway Traffic Safety Administration, keeps track of traffic accidents and lets people know if their cars have problems that carmakers need to fix.

DEPARTMENT OF LABOR

Role: Keeping people safe in the workplace and making sure their bosses treat them fairly. "Labor" is another word for "work," and this department works to help workers. This includes making sure businesses don't hire kids who are legally too young to work. One of the Labor Department's bureaus keeps track of the number of Americans who are working, what these workers are paid, and the cost of common goods and services.

Laboring Away
The department has made videos explaining labor laws that feature Batman and Batgirl, the Flintstones, and movie stars.

DEPARTMENT OF HEALTH AND HUMAN SERVICES (HHS)

Role: Helps keep Americans healthy. Its scientists and doctors study ways to prevent disease or help people who are already sick. One of its agencies, the Food and Drug Administration, makes sure new medicines are safe.

DEPARTMENT OF HOUSING AND URBAN DEVELOPMENT (HUD)

Role: Helps everyone get access to housing they can afford and makes sure landlords treat renters fairly. HUD gives some renters money to find the right home or apartment.

Home Sweet Home
Money from HUD helps provide housing to more than four million American families.

LAST BUT NOT LEAST!

These departments were the last ones to be created. They carry out a number of very important duties. Here's a look at their top responsibilities.

DEPARTMENT OF VETERANS AFFAIRS (VA)

Role: Helps veterans (vets), the folks who served in the U.S. military, after their service ends. The VA provides medical care for about nine million vets each year and handles other benefits for veterans, such as loans to buy homes.

DEPARTMENT OF EDUCATION

Role: Works to ensure all students have access to the best education possible. It does this in part by working with states and organizations to improve local schools. The department also provides loans and grants to help students attend college.

Class Dismissed
The country first had a Department of Education in 1867, but it lasted only one year. Some Americans feared it would have too much control over local schools.

DEPARTMENT OF HOMELAND SECURITY

Role: Created after terrorists attacked the United States on September 11, 2001, killing almost 3,000 people, its mission is to keep the country safe. Homeland Security includes the officers who screen people before they board planes, as well as the Coast Guard, which protects our shores, and the Secret Service. This service's main job is no secret—it protects the president, vice president, their families, and candidates running for those executive positions.

Super Gig
Department members help provide security at the *Super Bowl* and other important events.

DEPARTMENT OF ENERGY

Role: Makes sure the country has all the power it needs. Keeping the United States running requires a lot of energy in all forms, from gas to wind and solar power. It also runs 17 national laboratories that do research on everything from new forms of energy to climate change.

BY THE NUMBERS
The Department of Energy runs a superfast supercomputer that can do 200,000 trillion calculations in one second. It would take one person more than six billion years to do that!

SUPER IMPORTANT AGENCIES

The executive branch includes more than 60 other independent agencies. Their roles run the gamut. Here are some examples:

★ The National Endowment for the Arts provides money for the arts, from poetry and plays to musicals and museums.

★ The Federal Election Commission enforces laws related to elections.

★ The National Science Foundation promotes science education and research.

★ The Federal Reserve operates the country's central bank.

Here's a look at some of the other agencies you might have heard of, and that may play a role in your daily life.

GEE, MAIL!

If someone sends you a letter, there's a good chance the United States Postal Service (USPS) will bring it to your house. The country's first postal service started in 1775, with Benjamin Franklin in charge. Today, even with so many people sending texts and emails, the USPS still delivers more than 425 million items every day! And most people give the Postal Service their stamp of approval—a 2020 poll showed that 91 percent of Americans like the service. That's a higher rating than any other government agency has received.

WHAT A BLAST (OFF)!

In 1969, NASA, short for the National Aeronautics and Space Administration, sent the first humans to the moon. Today, it launches spacecraft that travel millions of miles to explore the planets and stars. NASA is also planning new missions to the moon as well as ones to more daring destinations, like Mars!

SOME OF THE UNUSUAL THINGS PEOPLE HAVE MAILED IN THE U.S. INCLUDE 80,000 BRICKS, A TREE TRUNK, AND A COCONUT!

SLY SPIES

When presidents want the scoop on what foreign countries are up to, they turn to the supersleuths at the Central Intelligence Agency (CIA). Its agents use technology to gather intelligence, or information, from around the world. Other times, CIA agents go undercover—meaning they pretend to be someone else—to learn what's happening overseas.

Psst, I've got intel!

Surprising Spies
CIA agents have included spy pigeons, and some agency dogs have been trained to sniff out bombs.

INFO FOR ALL

The Federal Communications Commission (FCC) regulates the companies that send out signals through the airwaves, over cable and telephone lines, and on the internet. The FCC's duties include making it easier for people all across the country to have access to fast internet connections. It also fights the spread of robocalls—those recorded phone messages that nobody asked for and everybody hates!

POLLUTION PATROL

The Environmental Protection Agency (EPA) was created in 1970. The EPA works to protect people and wildlife from harmful air, water pollution, and dangerous chemicals. At times, this means helping to clean up sites that are already polluted, along with stopping the pollution before it does damage.

CLEAN IT UP!
In 1969, folks in Cleveland, Ohio, saw a bizarre sight—the local river was on fire! Some oil-soaked items in the water had caught fire when struck by sparks from a nearby train. Such extreme pollution was one reason the EPA was created.

73

The Judicial BRANCH

Federal courts play a big role in the United States. The judicial branch hears cases when someone is accused of breaking a federal law, as well as some civil cases (meaning between two or more citizens). The person in charge of these trials is a judge. They make sure lawyers follow the rules of the court, including what kind of questions they can ask witnesses and what kind of evidence they can present. Judges are not supposed to take sides.

THE HIGHEST COURT

The U.S. Constitution created only one court—the Supreme Court of the United States, or SCOTUS for short. (The Constitution did give Congress the power to create other federal courts. You can read about them on page 80.)

The Supreme Court is like the ultimate decider. Most cases that reach SCOTUS have already been tried in lower courts, but someone involved disagreed with the decision.

JUSTICE JAMES F. BYRNES NEVER GRADUATED FROM HIGH SCHOOL. HE LATER TAUGHT HIMSELF LAW AND WAS APPOINTED TO THE SUPREME COURT.

When this happens, the person files an appeal, asking the Supreme Court to review it. Most of these cases raise an issue related to the Constitution. Other cases address legal conflicts between the United States and foreign countries or between individual U.S. states.

The members of the Supreme Court are called justices, which distinguishes them from regular judges. The court is led by the Chief Justice. While all the justices *might* agree on how to decide a case, they often have different views on how to interpret a law or part of the Constitution. That leads to split decisions.

The Constitution has no requirements for who can sit on the Supreme Court. A justice doesn't even have to be a lawyer! But so far, all of them have studied law before joining the Court. Unless a justice dies, resigns, or is impeached, they can serve for life. When a seat on the Court is vacant, the president gets to appoint a new member, but the Senate has to approve the choice. The Court started with six justices. Today, there are nine SCOTUS members, but Congress can change this number if it wants.

LOOKING TO THE PAST

The Supreme Court, and other courts, base many of their decisions on precedent. "Precedent" means how things have been done previously. To do this, justices look at other court cases similar to the one they are currently hearing. The decisions from those old cases shape their decision for the new case. But the Court might overturn a precedent if new facts show that the old case was not decided correctly. And if the two cases are not as similar as it first seems, the justices can ignore the precedent.

Nice try.

A FAMOUS CASE

In 1801, President John Adams named Virginia lawyer John Marshall the Chief Justice of the United States. Two years later, in a case called *Marbury* v. *Madison*, Marshall introduced the idea of judicial review—SCOTUS could decide that laws or executive orders were unconstitutional, meaning they violated the Constitution. Today, the Supreme Court often finds that state or federal laws aren't constitutional. Being able to toss out laws gives the Supreme Court a lot of its power.

SUPREMELY IMPORTANT DECISIONS

Some Supreme Court decisions have been super important in shaping life in the United States. Here's a look at a few of them.

PLESSY v. FERGUSON, 1896

The Civil War ended slavery, but African Americans still faced laws that restricted their rights, especially in the South. Schools and many public places were segregated, meaning Black people couldn't use the same services as white people. In *Plessy* v. *Ferguson*, SCOTUS ruled that segregation was allowed, as long as the services or schools were the same for both races. This idea was known as "separate but equal." In reality, things were hardly equal for Black communities.

KOREMATSU v. UNITED STATES, 1944

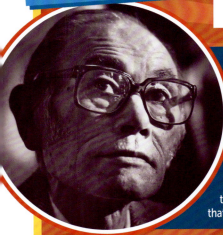

Japan bombed Pearl Harbor, Hawaii, in December 1941. The United States then went to war with Japan. Fearing many Japanese Americans might not be loyal to the country, the U.S. government sent more than 120,000 of them to camps where they were held prisoner. Fred Korematsu was a U.S. citizen who refused to report to a camp. He said the order was unconstitutional. The Court ruled against him, deciding that during wartime the government could take extreme measures to keep the country safe. Decades later, however, lawyers revealed that the government had hid or destroyed evidence proving that Japanese Americans weren't a threat to national security.

BROWN v. BOARD OF EDUCATION, 1954

In 1954, after Black people in several states challenged segregation in their local schools, SCOTUS overturned its decision in the *Plessy* v. *Ferguson* case, ruling that "separate but equal" education violated part of the 14th Amendment guaranteeing equal protection of all Americans under the law. The 9–0 decision spurred the effort to end segregation more broadly.

Words of Wisdom

"We conclude that, in the field of public education, the doctrine of 'separate but equal' has no place. Separate educational facilities are inherently unequal."

—Chief Justice Earl Warren

UNITED STATES v. NIXON, 1974

In 1973, a government-appointed lawyer, called a special prosecutor, was investigating if President Richard Nixon had committed a crime. The prosecutor wanted the president to hand over tape recordings he had secretly made in the White House. Nixon said no, arguing that a president has a special right called executive privilege, meaning he could refuse the demand. The Court ruled that a president does have executive privilege in *some* cases, but not when it comes to withholding evidence during a criminal investigation. Nixon eventually turned over the tapes. He resigned shortly after to avoid facing impeachment by Congress.

THE SUPREME COURT CASE ONE 1958 PLYMOUTH SEDAN v. COMMONWEALTH of PENNSYLVANIA SOUNDS LIKE A CAR SUED A STATE! IT WAS ACTUALLY THE CAR'S OWNER WHO SUED— AND WON!

OBERGEFELL v. HODGES, 2015

Before 2015, several states said that a married couple consisted of only a man and woman, and they would not allow same-sex couples to marry. The states also refused to recognize same-sex weddings performed in other states. Several same-sex couples then challenged their states' restrictions on same-sex marriage. The Supreme Court found that same-sex couples in every state have a constitutional right to marry, under the 14th Amendment. The justices ruled that the amendment gives everyone the right to marry, and LGBTQ Americans could not be denied the rights given to other Americans.

STARS IN COURT

et's meet some of the most famous "legal eagles" who have served on the Supreme Court.

EARL WARREN (1953–1969)

Earl Warren was a Republican named to the bench by a Republican president. But as Chief Justice, he surprised people with decisions that went against what many Republicans wanted. Like Thurgood Marshall, Warren played a huge role in *Brown* v. *Board of Education*. He convinced other justices to join his decision so the Court would rule unanimously against "separate but equal."

THURGOOD MARSHALL (1967–1991)

President Lyndon B. Johnson named Thurgood Marshall the first Black Supreme Court justice in 1967, but Marshall knew his way around the Supreme Court Building long before he became a justice. As a lawyer, he argued 32 cases before the Court. He won 29 of them, including *Brown* v. *Board of Education*. Marshall believed the federal government had a duty to protect the rights of Black Americans and other people of color.

I make it look easy.

SANDRA DAY O'CONNOR (1981–2006)

Sandra Day O'Connor showed her legal smarts when she finished law school in two years instead of the usual three. She served as a lawyer, assistant attorney general, and state senator in her native Arizona before President Ronald Reagan appointed her to the Supreme Court. O'Connor made history as the first woman justice. She was known for carefully considering the facts in every case and trying to win support from the other justices for her views.

Ruth Bader Ginsburg
(1993-2020)

Ruth Bader Ginsburg first found legal fame when she won cases before the Supreme Court that expanded legal rights for women. She continued to push for women's rights for her whole term as justice. By the time she died at the age of 87, Ruth Bader Ginsburg, known as RBG, was famous for her accomplishments. A movie and documentary were made about her life.

Antonin Scalia
(1986-2016)

Antonin Scalia served in the U.S. government, taught law, and was a federal judge before joining the Court. He was famous for his writing skills, which he often featured in dissenting opinions, and for his sense of humor. Scalia was known as an originalist. This means he tried to understand what the Founders were thinking as they wrote the Constitution. He then used those ideas to shape his decisions.

Sonia Sotomayor
(2009-PRESENT)

When Sonia Sotomayor moved from Puerto Rico to New York City with her family, she never dreamed she would become the first Hispanic American to serve on the U.S. Supreme Court! In 1991, Sotomayor became a federal district court judge. In one of her famous cases, she ruled in favor of major league baseball players who thought team owners should be called "Out!" for treating them unfairly. In 2009, President Barack Obama appointed Sotomayor to the Supreme Court. She's known for the clear writing style of her decisions.

Fitting the Bill

John Marshall and Salmon P. Chase are the only Supreme Court justices ever pictured on American money. Marshall was on the $500 bill, and Chase was on the $10,000. Neither of these big bills is used today.

Federal Courts OF ALL SORTS

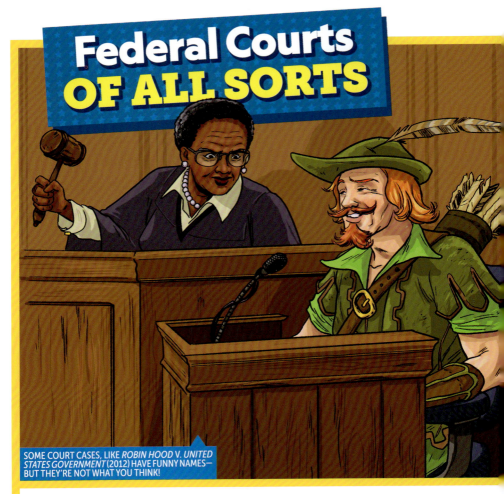

SOME COURT CASES, LIKE *ROBIN HOOD* V. *UNITED STATES GOVERNMENT* (2012) HAVE FUNNY NAMES—BUT THEY'RE NOT WHAT YOU THINK!

The Supreme Court is sometimes called the high court. There are also lower courts, where many cases go before they reach SCOTUS. Let's learn more about the two main systems of lower federal courts created by Congress.

STRICTLY DISTRICTS

At the lowest level are the district courts, where people go on trial if they're accused of breaking a federal law, such as selling or possessing illegal drugs. These courts may also hear cases when a person in one state sues someone in another state. More details about the district courts follow.

★ The country has 94 district courts, and each one has one or more judges.

★ All districts but one have their own U.S. attorneys called prosecutors—or government lawyers who present evidence to prove that someone committed a crime.

- District courts also handle civil cases involving the federal government. For example, the government awards patents for new inventions. This gives inventors the right to sell their creations. An inventor can sue in district court if someone else tries to sell their invention without permission.
- The country also has several special district courts that handle specific issues such as taxes and international trade.
- Both district judges and U.S. attorneys are appointed by the president and must be confirmed by the Senate.
- District judges, like SCOTUS justices, can serve for as long as they live. They can be impeached and removed from their job if they break the law or rules that judges must follow.
- U.S. attorneys serve for four years, though a president can choose to remove them before their term ends.

VERY APPEALING

Circuit courts, also sometimes called courts of appeals or appellate courts, make up the next level of the judiciary branch. The United States has 12 circuits, and they hear cases that have been appealed after a district court decision. The number of judges in a circuit varies from six to 29. Usually, only three of a circuit court's judges will hear an appeal. Lawyers on both sides submit written information explaining why they think the district court's decision should or shouldn't be overturned. They also appear before the judges to further explain their arguments and answer questions. In some cases, after the three-judge panel makes a decision, the case can be heard again by all the judges in the circuit.

HISTORICALLY, APPELLATE COURTS HAVE SOMETIMES BEEN CALLED THE COURT OF ERRORS.

SILLY-SOUNDING CASES

For the people waging a legal battle, there's nothing funny about going to court. But sometimes the names of the cases can bring a chuckle. Here are a few:

ROBIN HOOD v. UNITED STATES GOVERNMENT (2012)

No, this isn't referring to the legendary hero who took from the rich and gave to the poor. This Robin Hood argued that he had not received fair treatment in an earlier court case. The decision was no good for Hood—a district court tossed his case out.

UNITED STATES v. FORTY BARRELS & TWENTY KEGS OF COCA-COLA (1911)

The Coca-Cola folks argued that the U.S. government had illegally seized their barrels and kegs of soda after the government had claimed the drink contained a harmful ingredient. Both a district and appellate court went with the famous soda company. The Supreme Court, though, later overturned those rulings.

BATMAN v. COMMISSIONER (1951)

This sounds like the story of two famed comic-book allies who had to settle a disagreement. Instead, it was the case of a farmer who claimed his 14-year-old son was a partner in his business to get a better deal on his taxes. The court agreed with the commissioner for internal revenue, and the farmer had to pay up.

I'm innocent, I swear!

HOW TO MAKE A LAW

One of the federal government's main missions is creating and enforcing laws, with the judiciary branch making sure that laws are followed correctly. But as you've learned, before a law becomes a law, it's first a bill. Here's a close-up of how that bill moves through the lawmaking process.

Old School
House members use a special electronic machine to vote, but senators still call out "yea" or "nay" to cast their vote.

NO-GO ON A VETO
A law passed in 1996 tried to give the president the power to veto specific parts of bills relating to taxes and government spending. Two years later, the Supreme Court said no to this "line-item veto." The Court said the Constitution does not allow presidents to pick and choose what parts of a law they like. They have to sign or veto the entire bill.

1 BILL INTRODUCED
A member of Congress introduces a bill, which is named either HR (House of Representatives) or S (Senate) to show where it was introduced. Then it's given a number.

2 FIRST COMMITTEE

The bill is assigned to a committee that addresses the topic of the bill. For example, a bill that gives aid to farmers would go to the Agriculture Committee. The committee members collect information related to the bill.

3 FIRST VOTE

If the committee votes to accept the bill, it goes back to the full House or Senate for debate. If the chamber where the bill was introduced gives it a thumbs-up, then the bill goes over to the other chamber.

4 SECOND COMMITTEE & VOTE
In that second chamber, the committee process starts all over again. If the bill gets the nod there, then the whole second chamber votes on it.

5 EDITS

When both chambers pass a bill, it goes to the president. But sometimes the bill looks a little different when it goes to the commander in chief. This is because one chamber might have added or taken something out in order to move it along. In many cases, that means members from each chamber form a committee to hammer out a bill that both the House and Senate will approve.

6 DECISION TIME

After a bill is passed, the president has to decide within 10 days (not counting Sundays) whether they are going to sign or veto the bill.

6a VETO

A veto means no. With a regular veto, the bill goes back to Congress. If two-thirds of the members in each chamber vote for the bill again, it becomes a law, even though the president didn't agree.

6b POCKET VETO

If Congress is not in session and the president doesn't take action, the result is the same as a veto: The bill is dead. This is called a pocket veto.

6c DEFAULT YES

The president takes no action in those 10 days, but if Congress is in session during that time, the bill automatically becomes law.

6d SIGN IT

The president signs the bill, which makes it a law.

SINCE 1789, U.S. PRESIDENTS HAVE VETOED MORE THAN 2,500 BILLS. FRANKLIN D. ROOSEVELT, WHO SERVED LONGER THAN ANY OTHER PRESIDENT, HOLDS THE RECORD WITH 635 VETOES.

FINISHING TOUCHES

So, what happens once Congress and the president put a law into place? The judiciary branch steps in if someone thinks the law violates the Constitution. The federal courts weigh in to see if they think the law should stand. If not, the law is no longer enforced. Congress, though, can look at the law again to see if it can be changed to make it constitutional.

Putting on the PRESSURE

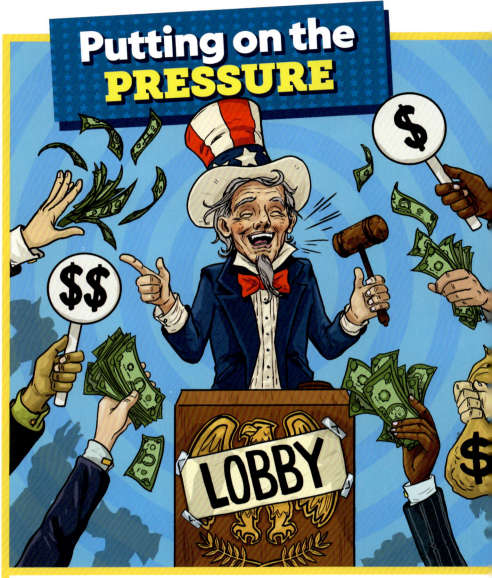

In politics, a lobby is a group of people who come together to try to shape government decisions. Lobbies often represent companies or groups with the same political goals. They range from businesses such as Amazon and Facebook to nonprofits like the Special Olympics and Boys & Girls Clubs of America.

THE WHO'S WHO OF LOBBYING

The people who work for a lobby are called lobbyists. Lobbyists try to convince members of Congress to support or oppose certain bills. Lobbyists also try to influence the president when they are considering whether to sign a bill.

Some companies and organizations have lobbyists on their staff. Others hire companies that do the lobbying for them. Government officials can take jobs with lobbying firms after they leave office, and lobbyists can sometimes take on government jobs.

Lobbying is a big business—groups trying to sway politicians spent almost four billion dollars in 2021 alone! More than a thousand different groups may try to lobby members of Congress on just one bill.

SHOW THEM THE MONEY

Lobbyists use their words to win over lawmakers. They show how a bill might benefit or harm Americans (and their lobby, too). But lobbies and lobbyists also try to win support by giving money to politicians when they seek office. The lobbyists hope that by giving this money, a politician will be more likely to back the bills their lobby likes.

GOOD LOBBYING ...

Lobbying is protected under the First Amendment. Companies and other groups have a right to express their views on important issues. And giving money to support the lawmakers who vote their way is considered a form of free speech. Lobbyists and the people who use them say that lobbying is good because it helps educate politicians on complex issues. Some lobbyists also push for laws designed to help large groups of people, such as laws that fight pollution or that try to protect women from violence.

... AND BAD

Some people think lobbies and their lobbyists have too much power and that some politicians will support whatever causes lobbyists give them lots of money to support. Large companies can spend more than other groups to shape laws that help only them and not average Americans. Other critics don't like that lobbyists who enter into government might be too cozy with the organizations they once lobbied for, since they can end up favoring the bills that lobby wants.

Another argument against lobbies is that government officials who leave office to take high-paying jobs as lobbyists can then try to use their connections with lawmakers to get certain laws passed. Former government workers are required to wait one or two years before influencing officials they used to work with, but many Americans would like to see former government officials wait even longer before they start lobbying.

LOBBYING IN THE LOBBY

Here's the lowdown on how "lobby" and "lobbyist" became common words in U.S. politics. Back in the early 1800s, one man who wanted to influence lawmakers in the New York legislature spent a lot of time in the building's lobby. A newspaper named him a "lobby member" of the legislature, compared to the actual members elected to serve. "Lobby member" and other related words soon appeared in newspapers across the country. The U.S. House of Representatives chamber in Washington, D.C., once had a lobby, too, where people could share their thoughts with lawmakers.

ONE GROUP LOBBIED FOR GIVING KIDS MORE RECESS IN SCHOOL!

A CAPITAL Idea

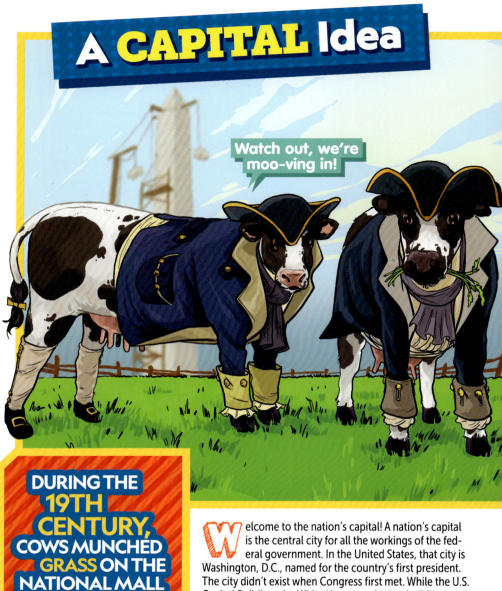

DURING THE 19TH CENTURY, COWS MUNCHED GRASS ON THE NATIONAL MALL AND PIGS ROAMED THE STREETS!

Welcome to the nation's capital! A nation's capital is the central city for all the workings of the federal government. In the United States, that city is Washington, D.C., named for the country's first president. The city didn't exist when Congress first met. While the U.S. Capitol Building, the White House, and other buildings were constructed, Philadelphia served as the capital city.

CREATING A CAPITAL

The Constitution called for creating a district, separate from the states, where a new capital city would be built. Maryland and Virginia donated part of their land for it. The location was another compromise for the Founders. Southern states thought it would be too easy for the northern states to dominate the new country if the capital remained in the North. Alexander Hamilton and other northern Founders then agreed to put the capital in the South.

Tree Huggers Unite
Washington is famous for its cherry trees, which blossom each spring. The more than 3,000 trees were sent in 1912 by the mayor of Tokyo, Japan. Each year, the capital hosts a month-long festival celebrating the trees that draws more than one million people.

President Washington chose the exact spot for the capital and picked a French architect named Pierre Charles L'Enfant to design the city. If you look at a map, you can see that most of the city's streets form a grid, with wider streets that run diagonally through the grid. Near the center of the city is Capitol Hill, the site of the Capitol Building. L'Enfant left plenty of room for public spaces. One of them is now called the National Mall. It's not a shopping mall—back then, a mall was an open space lined with trees where people would gather. The National Mall has been the site of countless protests, rallies, and celebrations. Many monuments have been built near the National Mall, including the Washington Monument, the Lincoln Memorial, and several memorials that honor Americans who fought in the country's major wars.

ON THE GROW
Washington, D.C., lost some of its land in 1847 when the area Virginia donated was returned to the state. Despite the loss of land, the city grew, and in 1901, leaders there started to plan major improvements, and building began on some of the memorials along the National Mall. Nearly 700,000 people call the nation's capital home. Many do not like the fact that they do not have voting rights in Congress. Washington, D.C., has major sports teams, and more than 24 million tourists visit the city every year.

So chic!

WHAT'S IN A NAME?
Before the capital was Washington, D.C., it was T.C.—Territory of Columbia. The name was changed in 1871. Columbia comes from Christopher Columbus. Before the American Revolution, the British at times called their American colonies Columbia. After the revolution, some Americans used the nickname for their new nation, too. The symbol for Columbia was a strong woman who was sometimes wrapped in a U.S. flag.

87

THAT'S MONUMENTAL

The nation's capital is filled with monuments and statues that honor notable Americans. Here are some of them.

LINCOLN MEMORIAL

The memorial for Abraham Lincoln is based on the design of the Parthenon, an ancient building in Athens, Greece. Inside the memorial is a statue of Honest Abe that stands 19 feet tall and weighs 175 tons. (That's nearly six meters and 160,000 kilograms!) On the walls are carved the words from two of his famous speeches: his second Inaugural Address and the Gettysburg Address.

THE WASHINGTON MONUMENT

Towering over the National Mall is this monument honoring George Washington. When it opened in 1888, the monument was the tallest building in the world. It's 555 feet 5 inches tall (just over 169 meters!), and visitors can take an elevator to the observation deck just below the monument's pointy peak. Stashed in a zinc box in one of the marble blocks at the monument's base are copies of the Declaration of Independence and Constitution, a U.S. flag, and an image of ol' George himself.

A SLOW BUILD

In 1854, builders constructing a monument to the first president of the United States hit a major snag—they ran out of money! A whopping 25 years later, the government resumed the project, but this time with marble from a different quarry. After years in the wind and rain, the stones have turned different colors, creating a distinct line in the stately structure.

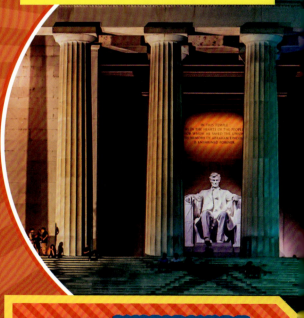

DURING A **WORLD WAR II** TRAINING DRILL, ARMY GUNNERS **ACCIDENTALLY FIRED THREE SHOTS** THAT HIT THE **LINCOLN MEMORIAL.** ONE OF THEM LEFT A HOLE ABOUT THE SIZE OF **A BASEBALL.**

JEFFERSON MEMORIAL

This memorial to Thomas Jefferson has a dome similar to one Jefferson designed for his home, Monticello, in Virginia. The area around the memorial is known for its cherry trees, which were a gift from Japan in 1912.

WORLD WAR II MEMORIAL

This memorial remembers the 16 million people who served in the U.S. military during World War II. More than 4,000 gold stars on the memorial honor the Americans who died during the war, with each star representing 100 people.

MARTIN LUTHER KING, JR. MEMORIAL

Martin Luther King, Jr., was one of the most important leaders of the civil rights movement, the effort to ensure that African Americans could vote and receive equal treatment under the law. More than 900 people or groups submitted plans for the memorial. The statue of King was carved by the Chinese sculptor Lei Yixin. The memorial opened in 2011.

Listen Up

Martin Luther King, Jr., gave his famous "I Have a Dream" speech on the steps of the Lincoln Memorial. Tens of thousands of marchers and leaders of the civil rights movement gathered to hear him speak.

GREAT DEBATE: SHOULD D.C. BE A STATE?

Washington, D.C., is a unique place. Though it isn't a state, people who live there can vote in the presidential election, and it has three electoral votes. The district doesn't have representatives or senators in Congress, but it does have a delegate who sits in the House. Even though this person can't vote on bills, they can still represent the views of D.C. residents. And, weirdly enough, until 1974, city voters couldn't choose their own elected officials. Until then, Congress ran the city. Today, Congress still reviews laws passed by the city council.

Some people in the capital and across the country think the current political setup is unfair for D.C. residents and have called for making Washington, D.C., the 51st state. But these efforts in Congress have, so far, failed. Some lawmakers say the city should stay as it is. Here are a few arguments for both sides.

D.C. RATES BEING A STATE

Like other Americans, Washington, D.C., residents pay a portion of the money they make at their jobs, called income taxes, to the federal government. For some, their call for statehood rests on an old idea—no taxation without representation! That's what the colonists demanded before the American Revolution, and the pro-state people say it should apply to them, too. They point out that D.C. residents pay more taxes than Americans in almost half the states do.

Statehood supporters also note that the district has a larger population than two states—Wyoming and Vermont—and about the same as several others. They think D.C. should have two senators and one representative to match these smaller states.

Some supporters also see the issue as important for African Americans. With its large Black population, D.C. could potentially elect Black senators and representatives if it achieved statehood. These members could speak out on issues that affect Black people across the country.

NO CHANGE!

People who think D.C. shouldn't be a state argue that they have the Constitution on their side. The article that called for creating a capital city said the district should be under the authority of Congress. Since Congress isn't allowed to govern the states, Congress would no longer control "the seat of the government," as the Constitution calls for. James Madison, for one, worried that if the nation's capital were a state, the residents there would have more influence over Congress than the residents of other states.

Words of Wisdom

"Virginia's neighbors in D.C. deserve representation just like every other American. It's far past time to … grant hundreds of thousands of taxpaying Americans this fundamental right."

—Tim Kaine, senator from Virginia

BY THE NUMBERS

In 2016, 86 percent of people in D.C. who voted in a special election, called a referendum, favored making the city a state.

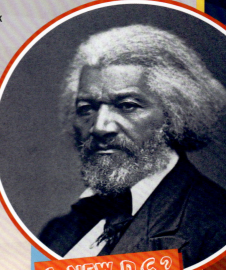

A NEW D.C.?

The House of Representatives recently passed a bill *twice* to make Washington, D.C., a state, but the Senate never voted on it. The bill would name the new state "Washington, Douglass Commonwealth," honoring Frederick Douglass, who escaped slavery in 1838 and worked to end it across the United States.

Words of Wisdom

"Our Founding Fathers explicitly set aside a federal district to serve as the seat of government. It was never intended to operate as a state, and for good reason …"

—Ken Paxton, attorney general of Texas

POTUS Is in THE HOUSE

George Washington got to pick the site of the capital city, but he missed out on visiting one of the country's landmarks—the White House. The presidential home wasn't completed until 1800; Washington died in 1799. John Adams was the first president to call the White House home, though work on the house was still not done when he and his wife, Abigail, moved in.

Here's a peek inside at some of the most famous parts of this historic house.

A Grand Place

The White House got its official name in 1901. Before that, people called it the President's Palace, the President's House, and the Executive Mansion.

THE WEST WING

This is where presidents and their staff work. The Oval Office (yes, it's really shaped like an oval!) is located there, and that's where the president really gets down to business. The vice president has an office in the West Wing, too.

PRIVATE RESIDENCE

The top two floors of the White House are where the president and president's family live. Their guests stay there, too, often in the room called the Lincoln Bedroom (Abraham Lincoln used the room as an office).

EAST ROOM

This large room was designed as a space to host and entertain visitors; it has seen its share of elegant dinners with important foreign guests. Presidents have also held concerts and dances here. John and Abigail Adams, however, had a slightly less fancy use for the room—hanging laundry to dry.

BY THE NUMBERS

The White House has 132 rooms and three elevators! It also has its own movie theater, so you can kick back and watch films in style.

THE ROSE GARDEN

This outdoor area is famous for—you guessed it—flowers. The garden's lawn can hold up to 1,000 guests when a president hosts visitors outside. Another garden at the White House is called the Children's Garden. This is a secluded spot just for kids, featuring the hand- and footprints of presidential grandchildren, which are set in bronze. Another popular outdoor spot for children is the South Lawn, where the president hosts the annual Easter Egg Roll.

REC ROOMS AND OTHER EXTRAS

The White House has a tennis court, a running track, a bowling alley, and a putting green for golfers to practice their game. At one point, the house also had an indoor pool in the basement. Today, the basement includes a kitchen and a flower shop and also leads to a special underground room called a bunker. The president can go there during emergencies when it's unsafe to be in the White House.

WHITE HOUSE FUN FACTS

Here are 10 surprising facts about the president's digs!

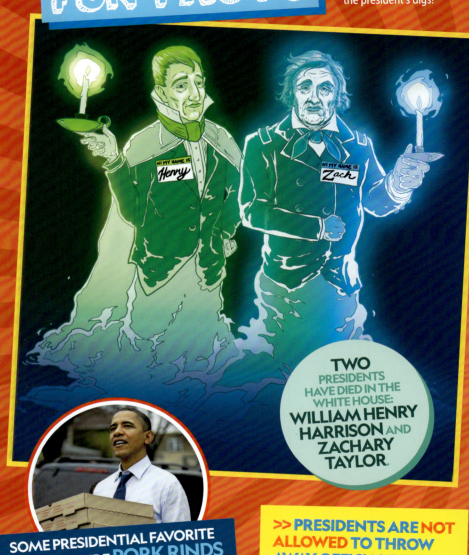

TWO PRESIDENTS HAVE DIED IN THE WHITE HOUSE: WILLIAM HENRY HARRISON AND ZACHARY TAYLOR.

SOME PRESIDENTIAL FAVORITE FOODS INCLUDE PORK RINDS (GEORGE H. W. BUSH), PIZZA (BARACK OBAMA), AND MEATLOAF (RICHARD NIXON). NIXON ALSO LIKED COTTAGE CHEESE WITH KETCHUP!

>> PRESIDENTS ARE NOT ALLOWED TO THROW AWAY OFFICIAL DOCUMENTS THEY RECEIVE OR DELETE EMAILS OR TEXTS RELATING TO THEIR OFFICIAL DUTIES.

WHITE HOUSE HISTORY

There's a lot more to know about America's most historic house and the people who have called it home. Let's dive in!

1792: Construction begins.

1814: The British burn the White House during the War of 1812.

1891: Electric lights are used for the first time. Before that, the halls were lit with gas lighting.

1800: John Adams is the first president to move in.

1902: The West Wing is added to the house.

1929: A fire on Christmas Eve damages part of the West Wing.

A HOUSE AFIRE

In 1812, the United States and Great Britain went to war. Two years later, British troops attacked Washington, D.C. Before fleeing the White House, First Lady Dolley Madison made a dash for the dining room. She ordered Paul Jennings, an enslaved Black teenager, to take a painting of George Washington from the wall because Madison didn't want enemy soldiers to destroy it. The painting commemorated the very first president, after all! She then gave it to two friends for safekeeping. After Madison ran for safety, British soldiers stormed the White House. They stole some items, then set the house on fire. The British also burned the U.S. Capitol and other buildings.

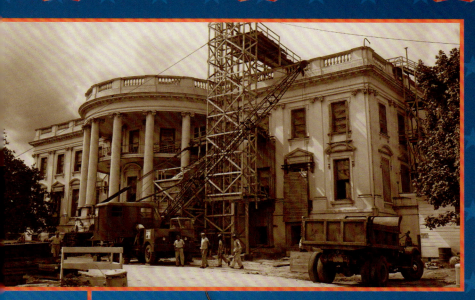

1948–1952: Because of the danger of it collapsing, due to old fire damage and many modifications over the years, almost the entire house is rebuilt.

1979: The first computer is installed.

1992: George H. W. Bush becomes the first president to use email.

1942: The East Wing is added; beneath it is the bunker used during emergencies.

2002: Solar panels are placed on part of the roof.

2017: More than 200 workers make renovations that include replacing old heating and cooling systems.

THE ENERGY FROM SOME OF THE SOLAR PANELS ON THE WHITE HOUSE ROOF POWERS A HOT TUB!

Home Away FROM HOME

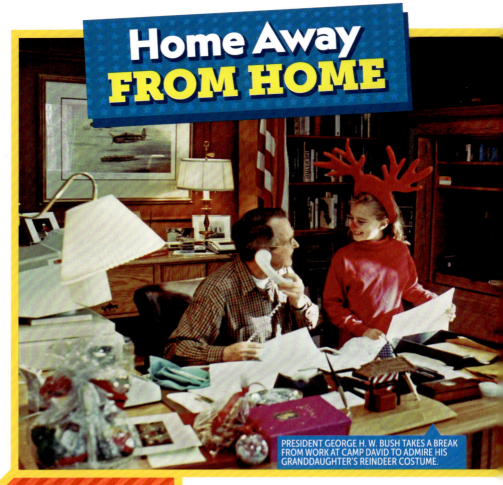

PRESIDENT GEORGE H. W. BUSH TAKES A BREAK FROM WORK AT CAMP DAVID TO ADMIRE HIS GRANDDAUGHTER'S REINDEER COSTUME.

PRESIDENTS AND THEIR GUESTS USE GOLF CARTS TO ZIP AROUND CAMP DAVID. GEORGE W. BUSH CALLED HIS "GOLF CART ONE."

Being POTUS is no easy feat, and sometimes the president needs to take a break. The president, their family, and guests can relax at Camp David, located in a woodsy area of Maryland about 60 miles (97 km) from Washington, D.C. A helicopter called Marine One transports the president to the camp. Unlike the White House, Camp David is not open to the public.

SUMMER COMFORT

Before Camp David became a presidential hideaway in 1942, it was a recreational area for federal workers. Then, as World War II was raging, President Franklin D. Roosevelt needed a safe spot where he could go to relax. He also liked that the location was about 10 degrees cooler (6°C) in the summer than hot and humid Washington, D.C. FDR called the camp Shangri-La, the name of a mythical paradise. The camp has a main house for the president and cabins for guests, who can stay there year-round, thanks to the heating that President Harry S. Truman added.

NEW NAME, NEW GAMES

In 1953, President Dwight D. Eisenhower renamed Shangri-La for his grandson, David. Eisenhower also installed a one-hole golf course where he could practice his swing. Over the years, presidents have added other features to Camp David. Today, it has a pool, tennis courts, a basketball court, a movie theater, a bowling alley, and a game room. Presidents have used the trails at the camp to jog and ride horses and mountain bikes.

TIME FOR BUSINESS

It's not all fun and games at Camp David. Presidents sometimes invite foreign leaders there, too, to discuss serious issues without being distracted. Other times, presidents bring their top advisers. After the 9/11 terrorist attacks, President George W. Bush took several Cabinet members there to decide how to respond. Most of the time, though, Camp David is a place where a president can unwind from one of the hardest jobs in the world.

A PEACEFUL PLACE

President Jimmy Carter hosted two foreign leaders at Camp David who used their stay to make history. In 1978, Israel's Menachem Begin and Egypt's Anwar Sadat spent almost two weeks at the camp trying to work out a peace agreement. Egypt and several other Arab nations had fought several wars with Israel since 1948. Carter worked with Begin and Sadat to create what are known as the Camp David Accords. Israel and Egypt agreed to sign a peace treaty the next year. They called on other nations in the region to also sign peace treaties with Israel.

INSIDE the CAPITOL

The U.S. Capitol is certainly a big, beautiful building! Along with the White House, it's one of the symbols of American democracy. But what are some of its unique features and what does it look like inside? Let's take a look!

DOME, SWEET DOME

The huge dome on top of the Capitol is easy to spot when strolling around downtown D.C. It is 287 feet (87 m) high, including the statue, called the Statue of Freedom, that sits on top. The dome is made out of cast iron—almost 4,500 tons (4,080 t) of it. That's equal to nearly nine million pounds (4,100,000 kg)! The iron has been painted to look the same as the stone building beneath it.

STATUE OF FREEDOM

At the tip-top of the Capitol dome is the Statue of Freedom. The bronze statue is almost 20 feet (6 m) tall and shows a woman wearing a helmet and clothing similar to what was worn in ancient Rome. In one hand, "Lady Freedom" holds a sword, and in the other, a shield with 13 stripes, one for each of the original states.

ROTUNDA

A rotunda is a round, open area in the middle of a building, often covered by a dome. The Capitol Rotunda is used for special events, such as honoring important Americans when they die. Look up and you'll see a painting of George Washington rising into the heavens, almost 200 feet (60 m) above the ground.

COMING CLEAN

During the 1850s, many senators rented rooms in Washington, D.C., that didn't have bathrooms. To help senators wash up, six marble bathtubs were placed in the basement of the Capitol. Senators sometimes chatted with each other or prepared speeches as they scrubbed up.

100

STATUARY HALL

This hall of statues was once used as the main House chamber, where representatives debated bills. The hall now features statues of famous Americans, with two from each state. But as the country grew, the hall wasn't able to hold all the statues. Today, there are 100 statues in the Capitol collection, 35 of which line the walls of this hall. The others are placed throughout the building.

THE SHAPE OF THE NATIONAL STATUARY HALL CREATES A "WHISPERING GALLERY"—IF YOU STAND IN THE RIGHT SPOT, YOU CAN EASILY HEAR SOMEONE TALKING FROM THE OTHER SIDE OF THE HALL.

HOUSE AND SENATE WINGS

Each chamber of Congress has its own wing in the Capitol. Both wings are filled with art showing scenes of American history. Beneath the House chamber is the Hall of Columns, which—you guessed it—is lined with columns. The hall is home to some of the statues that are part of the Statuary Hall collection.

TUNNELS OF GOV

There's a whole other world beneath the Capitol. It sits on Capitol Hill, which has offices for members of Congress, as well as the Supreme Court Building and the Library of Congress. Representatives and senators ride their own mini-subways to get to and from the Capitol, and tunnels connect many of the buildings on the Hill.

Not Just ANY LIBRARY

THE LIBRARY OF CONGRESS JEFFERSON BUILDING

The Capitol was once the home of the Library of Congress. The library got its own building in 1897. Like the Capitol and other federal buildings, the design of the library was partly shaped by architecture found in ancient Greece and Rome. It has columns like those on ancient temples, and a fountain in front of the library features Neptune, the Roman god of the sea.

The library's first building is named for Thomas Jefferson. His books—more than 6,000 of them!—formed a big part of the library's early collection. A second building named for John Adams opened in 1939, and a third named for James Madison opened in 1980. The Library of Congress is the largest library in the world.

ANYONE 16 OR OLDER CAN USE THE LIBRARY, BUT THEY CAN'T TAKE ITEMS FROM THE BUILDING.

KEEPING RECORDS

An archive is a place that collects important documents of all kinds. The National Archives and Records Administration (NARA) is in charge of the U.S. government's archives and keeps some of its most important records.

Like the Library of Congress, the Archives collects maps, pictures, film, sound recordings, and more. It now even collects digital government records, too. The Archives has more than 13 billion paper records, along with millions of photos, electronic data like emails, and other information. At the National Archives Museum in Washington, D.C., visitors can see originals of some of the most important documents in U.S. history, including the Declaration of Independence and the Constitution. There's even the check from 1867 that the U.S. government used to pay for Alaska!

BY THE NUMBERS

Number of books, magazines, recordings, and other items in the Library of Congress: **more than 173 million**

New items received every day: **15,000**

Foreign languages represented in its stacks: **about 470**

Smallest book: about the size of this dot .

Largest book: **5 by 7 feet (1.5 m by 2.1 m)**

Presidents with personal papers held in the library: **23**

Visual images (pictures, posters, maps, etc.): more than **17 million; more than 1.2 million are available online**

Sound recordings: **more than 4.2 million**

Number of visits to the library website: **178.1 million between October 1, 2020, and September 30, 2021**

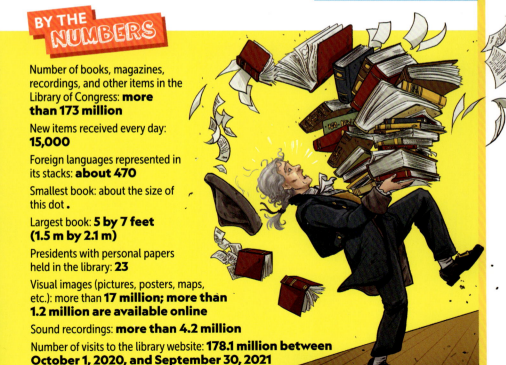

MUSEUMS AND MORE

You can learn even more about the country's history at the Smithsonian Institution. It has 19 museums, with two more on the way, and places where people do research on everything from the environment to American art. The National Zoo is part of the institution, too. Members of the federal government, including the vice president and the Chief Justice of the United States, help manage the Smithsonian, along with some private citizens. Here's a look at just some of what the Smithsonian offers.

NATIONAL MUSEUM OF AFRICAN AMERICAN HISTORY AND CULTURE

This museum, one of the newer parts of the Smithsonian, traces Black history from the days of slavery to present day. Different exhibits look at the role African Americans have played in art, sports, and the military, and at their political struggle to win equal rights.

NATIONAL AIR AND SPACE MUSEUM

You'll be over the moon with all the great air and space stuff on display here. The museum has the first U.S. spacecraft to orbit Earth, the first airplane flown by the Wright brothers in 1903, and many more historic aircraft. You can even touch a moon rock that astronauts brought back to Earth!

104

NATIONAL MUSEUM OF THE AMERICAN INDIAN

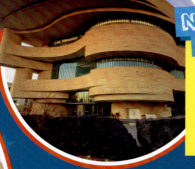

This museum explores the history, art, and religions of the people who came to North America thousands of years before Europeans knew the continent existed. It has one of the world's largest collections of items relating to Native American culture. Part of the museum looks at the U.S. government's relationship with tribal nations.

NATIONAL MUSEUM OF NATURAL HISTORY

You can learn about mummies, mammals, minerals, and more at this museum. Its exhibits also let you explore the oceans, get info on insects, see skeletons, and dig into dinosaurs. This is the largest collection of natural history items in the world. But not everything is about the past—the museum also looks at issues Earth faces today, such as climate change.

Come visit me!

Did You Know?
The Museum of Natural History's Hope Diamond is the largest known blue diamond and is said to be worth at least $350 million!

NATIONAL MUSEUM OF AMERICAN HISTORY

The flag that inspired the "Star-Spangled Banner," boxing gloves worn by Muhammad Ali, dresses from the first ladies—all these and more are under one roof. The museum has almost two million items that showcase the country's history.

SMITHSONIAN INSTITUTION BUILDING

You'll get the royal treatment at the Smithsonian's visitors center. It's nicknamed the Castle because it reminds some people of one. The building dates from 1855. Inside, you can see highlights from the other Smithsonian offerings.

ON DISPLAY

The important buildings in the nation's capital can seem endless. Here are a few other places, sometimes open to the public, where government work goes on.

THE SUPREME COURT BUILDING

It wasn't until 1935 that SCOTUS got its own building, and it was worth the wait. The Supreme Court Building is another excellent example of how Roman architecture influenced American builders. With some planning, visitors are able to hear the justices of the Supreme Court at work, and to explore the courtroom when court is not in session.

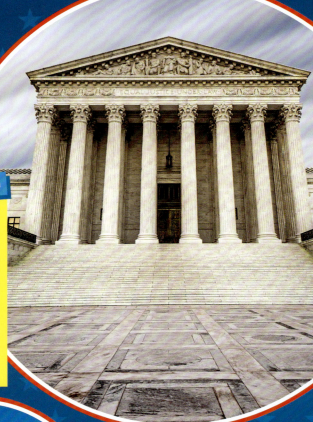

FEDERAL BUREAU OF INVESTIGATION (FBI)

Some of the FBI's 35,000 special agents and staff work at the bureau's headquarters in the capital. Visitors can schedule a tour of part of the building to learn about the FBI's work, as well as how agents find and examine evidence, rescue people who are held hostage, and nab computer criminals.

BUREAU OF ENGRAVING AND PRINTING

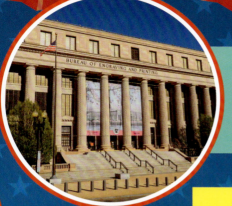

If you want someone to show you the money, this is the place to go. This bureau is in charge of designing and printing all the paper money used in the United States. When tours of the building are being offered, you can even see real money being printed.

THE PENTAGON

The Department of Defense's headquarters is located just outside of Washington, D.C., in Arlington, Virginia. The building's name refers to its five sides and comes from the Greek word for "five." It took more than 15,000 workers to build it in just 16 months. The Pentagon is huge—it has 7,754 windows and more than 17 miles (27 km) of hallways. On a tour, visitors walk about 1.5 miles (2.4 km) of those hallways. You can learn about the history of the U.S. military and see a tribute to the people who died there on September 11, 2001. The Pentagon was one of the targets of the terrorist attacks that day.

SPY STUFF

There's one museum connected to the federal government you can visit only online: the museum of the Central Intelligence Agency (CIA). Visitors aren't allowed at the CIA's headquarters in Langley, Virginia, for security reasons. So, the agency did the next best thing and created a virtual museum online, where you can see the tricks and tools of the spy trade. It includes a hollow silver dollar used to carry secret messages; a tiny radio receiver hidden in a pipe; spy cameras that use tiny pieces of film; and Charlie, a robot fish used to collect water samples.

I'm built to last!

U.S. **DOLLAR BILLS** ARE ACTUALLY MADE OF **COTTON** AND **LINEN**. THEY'RE DESIGNED TO BE ABLE TO WITHSTAND **4,000** DOUBLE FOLDS (FORWARD AND BACK)!

107

Shh ... This Section IS FULL OF SECRETS

Sometimes the government chooses to keep things secret. Different agencies share their projects with only a few people, and some of that information may be classified. This means people need special permission, or clearance, to see it.

SECRET POWERS

As you'd expect, many of the projects Americans know little or nothing about relate to the military and intelligence. One of the most secretive agencies in recent times has been the National Security Agency (NSA), which is part of the Department of Defense. The NSA can listen in on phone calls and read emails from around the world. For a time, the government wouldn't admit that this agency existed.

Secret Spaces

When the president needs to look at and talk about secret information, they head to a special space called a sensitive compartmented information facility (SCIF). The government has strict rules for setting up SCIFs. They should have few or no windows and, if possible, soundproof rooms so no one outside can hear what's said. Many also have armed guards outside. The goal is to make it hard for spies to find out what is discussed inside a SCIF.

Other parts of the Department of Defense keep secrets, too. This is especially true when it comes to new weapons. Some programs are so secret only a few members of Congress are told about them.

SECRET'S OUT

Over time, word of some of the government's secret programs can get out. In some cases, the government itself finally talks—but only after receiving tough questions from Congress. That was the case with the CIA. In 1975, the agency admitted that for several decades it had illegally investigated U.S. citizens and was involved in attempts, sometimes successful, to kill foreign leaders.

One "secret weapon" that didn't stay a secret for long is the SR-71, a spy plane also called the Blackbird. President Lyndon Johnson confirmed the plane's existence in 1964, after newspapers began to ask questions about secret tests in Utah. With a top speed of about 2,200 miles an hour (3,540 km/h), it was the fastest plane ever—nearly four times faster than your average airplane! It was also a high flier, reaching altitudes of about 85,000 feet (25,900 m). The Blackbird flew too high and fast to be shot down, and its powerful cameras were able to take pictures of the ground below.

NOT-SO-HIDDEN HIDEAWAY

Another secret the world now knows is that, starting in the late 1950s, the government built a bomb shelter underneath the Greenbrier, a fancy hotel in West Virginia, as a hiding place for members of Congress. The bunker is 720 feet (219 m) belowground, and it took 50,000 tons (that's 45,000,000 kg!) of concrete to build it. At one point, the government stored enough food there to feed 1,000 people for two months. A Washington, D.C., newspaper reported the existence of the bunker in 1992 after talking to some of the people who had helped build it.

THE NSA'S SUPERCOMPUTERS USE FIVE MILLION GALLONS (19 MILLION L) OF RECYCLED WASTEWATER PER DAY TO KEEP FROM OVERHEATING!

Strange things are out there!

For years, many Americans have wondered whether alien spaceships are zipping around Earth—or maybe even landing on our planet. In 1947, there were reports of a "flying saucer" crashing near Roswell, New Mexico. Some people even claimed the government had found the bodies of aliens in the crash. For decades after, U.S. officials didn't say much about "unidentified flying objects," or UFOs for short. Then, in 2021, the government issued a report: It didn't say if alien spaceships are real or not, but it did say there are reports of "unidentified aerial phenomena" (UAP) that it can't explain. The Pentagon also created a new office to study UAP, but many people think that if government officials learn that aliens are visiting Earth, they'll keep it secret.

Join the PARTY!

COLOR ME RED— OR BLUE

States are sometimes called red or blue, depending on which party typically gets its electoral votes. Red is for Republicans, and blue is for Democrats. The colors came about during the presidential election in 2000, when on a map of the U.S., news outlets used red to mark states that voted for Republican George W. Bush and blue for ones that backed Al Gore, the Democrat. Was there some secret formula for choosing the colors? Nope—Republicans got red because both words begin with *R*. Today, swing states are called purple (get it? A mix of blue and red), since they don't always go for the same party.

A political party is a group of people who have similar ideas and opinions about how the government should be run, the types of laws politicians should make, and what the government's role in society should be. These parties work to get candidates they support elected. Today, the Democratic and Republican Parties call many of the shots in the federal government. Which laws get passed and how they're enforced can depend on the party controlling Congress and the White House. And when control of these two branches is split between the two main parties, it can be hard for much to get done.

PARTY? HARDLY!

The Constitution doesn't mention political parties, and many of the Founders didn't like the idea that people might form them. George Washington worried that powerful people would take over a party and do what was best for them, instead of the whole country. Washington spoke out against parties in 1796, but he was too late—the first two political parties had already formed. And by then, members of both parties already thought the other was up to no good.

Two members of Washington's Cabinet became the unofficial leaders of the first parties. Secretary of the Treasury Alexander Hamilton led the Federalists, who wanted a strong federal government with a national bank. Federalists thought the government should help businesses and industries grow.

On the other side were the Anti-Federalists, who later joined the Democratic-Republican Party, led by Secretary of State Thomas Jefferson. They wanted to limit the power of the federal government and thought agriculture should drive the U.S. economy.

THE PARTY'S OVER

For a while, Jefferson's party had control. By the time James Monroe became president in 1817, the country was said to be in an "era of good feelings," a time when the national mood was positive, united, and optimistic about the future. Even old Federalists agreed with many of the Democratic-Republicans' policies. But the good feelings didn't last, and over the next few decades, new parties began to form. Over time, the goals of some political parties began to change, too. Today, the Democratic and Republican Parties have very different goals from when they were founded.

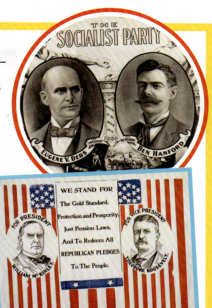

Wait, I thought this was a party!

HOW MAJOR PARTIES GOT STARTED

NAME	FOUNDED	ORIGINAL GOAL
Federalist	1795	strong national government
Democratic-Republican	1796	more power for the states (states' rights)
Democratic	1828	states' rights and power for average citizens
Whig	1834	reduce presidential power
Republican	1854	stop expansion of slavery
Socialist	1901	promote rights of workers, weaken power of businesses
Libertarian	1971	reduce power of the government
Green	1984	protect the environment, promote social justice and peace
Constitution	1992	limit powers of the federal government

Party People: DEMOCRATS

I'm honored!

SOME PEOPLE THOUGHT **ANDREW JACKSON** WAS AS **STUBBORN AS A DONKEY.** DEMOCRATS WEREN'T INSULTED— THEY MADE A DONKEY THEIR **PARTY SYMBOL!**

Symbol: Donkey
Color: Blue
Founded in: 1828
Also known as: "the Left" or "Liberals"

Who they are: People within the Democratic Party have many different views—they don't all think the same about every issue. But generally, Democrats seek to limit the power of big businesses, to support federal regulation of businesses, and to create and maintain federally funded assistance programs to help citizens. Democrats think individual rights should be protected at the federal level. The Democratic Party is also in favor of creating laws that protect the environment, for example, by reducing the use of fossil fuels that contribute to climate change.

112

MEMORABLE DEMOCRATS

Democrat Geraldine Ferraro was the first female vice presidential candidate. She ran with presidential candidate Walter Mondale in 1984.

Democrats were in the White House for the longest consecutive stretch of time—for 20 years—during the presidencies of Franklin D. Roosevelt and Harry S. Truman.

Democratic president Barack Obama was the first African American president (term: 2009–2017). He was also the first president to have a Twitter account!

When she took office in 2019, Alexandria Ocasio-Cortez was just 29 years old—the youngest woman ever to serve in Congress.

Democratic president Woodrow Wilson (term: 1913–1921) was the last president to take a horse and carriage to an inauguration.

Democratic president Jimmy Carter (term: 1977–1981) could speed-read at a rate of 2,000 words a minute.

Party People: REPUBLICANS

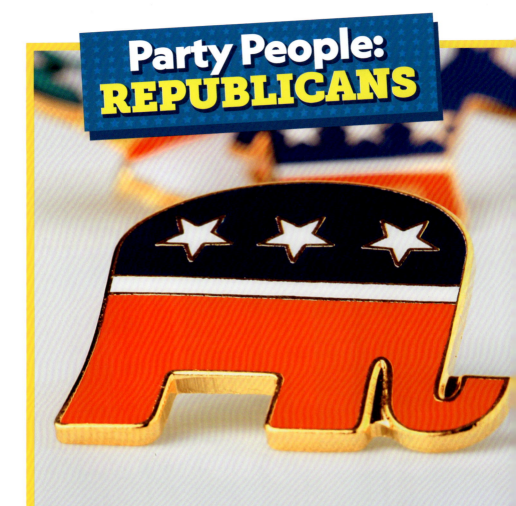

THE REPUBLICANS CHOSE AN ELEPHANT AS THE SYMBOL FOR THEIR PARTY IN THE LATE 1800S AFTER A CARTOONIST ASSOCIATED ITS SUPPORTERS WITH THE ANIMAL!

Symbol: Elephant
Color: Red
Founded in: 1854
Also known as: "the Right" or "Conservatives"
Who they are: People within the Republican Party also have many different views—they don't all think the same about every issue. But generally, Republicans wish to reduce the national debt, have a strong national defense, and limit government control. The Republican Party is also typically in favor of a stricter interpretation of the U.S. Constitution.

Red is my best color!

MEMORABLE REPUBLICANS

The first Republican president was Abraham Lincoln (term: 1861–65). He was also the tallest president at six feet four inches (2 m). He towered over people and added more height with his iconic "stovepipe" top hats. He was even known to keep important documents under them.

Republican president Benjamin Harrison (term: 1889–1893) was the first president to live in the White House after electricity had been installed there, but he was so afraid of getting electrocuted that he never touched the light switches.

Republican president Theodore Roosevelt (term: 1901–09) was the first president to fly in an airplane, and the first to dive in a submarine.

Republican president Ronald Reagan (term: 1981–89) had a bad habit. He smoked. To help him quit, he started eating jelly beans instead. Jelly Belly was his go-to candy brand, and the company supplied him with enough jelly beans to last him through all eight years of his presidency. His favorite flavor was licorice.

Republican president George W. Bush (term: 2001–09) loved to run, so he kept a treadmill on Air Force One and ran during flights.

115

More Than TWO CAN PLAY

MILLARD **FILLMORE** AND MARTIN **VAN BUREN** ARE THE ONLY OTHER **FORMER PRESIDENTS** WHO LATER RAN AS THIRD-PARTY CANDIDATES. **BOTH LOST.**

Either a Democrat or a Republican has called the White House home since 1853. But in many presidential elections, candidates from other parties throw their hats into the ring, too. None of them has ever won, but a few have had success in winning votes.

TEDDY TRIES AGAIN

After serving almost two terms in the White House, Theodore Roosevelt ran again in 1912. But that time, the Republicans didn't choose him as their candidate. That didn't stop Roosevelt. He formed his own party, called the Progressives. The party became better known as the Bull Moose Party after Roosevelt told reporters he felt as strong as a bull moose. Roosevelt did better than any other third-party candidate before or since, coming in second.

POPULAR VOTES: 4.1 million
ELECTORAL VOTES: 88

DEBS THE BREAKS

Eugene Debs wasn't giving up without a fight. Starting in 1900, he ran for president five times—the last time while he was in jail! He had been convicted of speaking out against America's role in World War I, which was a crime at the time. Debs belonged to the Socialist Party, which wanted to give workers more rights and have the government control most large industries. He won more votes in 1920, when he was behind bars, than in his other races.

POPULAR VOTES (1920): 919,799
ELECTORAL VOTES: 0

RUNNING ON RACE

In 1968, the United States was fighting a war in Vietnam. At home, violence was on the rise in many cities. Some voters believed the two major parties weren't doing well with the big issues at the time, including the war. They found a candidate they liked better in former Alabama governor George Wallace of the newly formed American Independent Party. Wallace had strongly supported segregation, and many of his supporters were white voters who were unhappy with the gains of the civil rights movement. His party's platform also called for giving states and towns more control over their own affairs. Wallace was the last third-party candidate to date to win electoral votes.

POPULAR VOTES: 9.9 million
ELECTORAL VOTES: 46

A FAMOUS FIRST

Victoria Woodhull had many claims to fame. She and her sister Tennie Claflin were the first American women to start a weekly newspaper. On her own, Woodhull scored another big first: In 1872, she was the first woman to run for president—before all American women could even vote! Woodhull's party hoped to change that and give women other legal rights as well. Woodhull's name never appeared on any state's ballot. Even if she had won enough to be elected, she wouldn't have been able to serve as president. She was 34, so she didn't meet the constitutional requirement that a president be at least 35 years old.

VOTER REGISTRATION TODAY

Democrats: 49.3 million
Republicans: 36.4 million
Independent/third party: 38.8 million

*Data as of 2021. Not all states require voters to register with a party.

Vote for me!

Win With **WALLACE** IN 1968

The Party's Pig

One small third party was the American Vegetarian Party, which called for people to stop eating meat. The Youth International Party of the 1960s nominated a pig as its candidate for president.

THE WRITE STUFF

In many states, voters can write in the name of someone who isn't on the ballot. In presidential races, some of the people getting these write-in votes have included football superstar Tom Brady, musician Bruce Springsteen, and former first lady Michelle Obama.

117

ON THE RUN

Running for elected office—and winning!—takes time and money, and that effort is called a campaign. Here's a look at how election campaigns typically work (though, keep in mind that rules vary from state to state).

1 MAKE IT OFFICIAL

Before a candidate throws their hat into the ring, they've already been hard at work. They usually have started to raise money and seek support from people who know them. In many races, the candidates hire staff to help spread their ideas. Often, that's by buying ads and creating social media accounts. Candidates rely on volunteers to do some of this work, too.

Yes, we can!

2 HIT THE TRAIL

Candidates then begin to meet with voters to win more support—and to raise more money. The heart of a campaign is convincing voters that one candidate is better than anyone else running for the same office.

SPREADING THE WORD

The internet has helped candidates connect with voters. Before the internet, candidates had to rely on less sophisticated communication, like catchy slogans such as "I like Ike" for Dwight D. Eisenhower. Some even had songs written about them! One toe-tapper, "Honest Old Abe," was composed to support Abraham Lincoln.

SOME OTHER CAMPAIGN SLOGANS INCLUDED "KEEP COOL WITH [CALVIN] COOLIDGE"; "ROSS FOR BOSS," FOR ROSS PEROT; AND "WELL, DEWEY OR DON'T WE?" FOR THOMAS DEWEY.

3 CONVENTION CONTENTION

When a party has two or more of its members seeking the same seat, it holds an event called a convention. Local party members choose delegates to represent them. The candidate who wins the most votes from the delegates is the party's endorsed, or preferred, candidate. But candidates who aren't endorsed can still keep running. Depending on the state, these candidates can often run in an election called a primary, which lets all party members choose their preferred candidate.

4 A PRIMARY EVENT

In a primary election, voters decide which candidates they want to have on the final ballot for the main event—the general election. States have different laws for how primaries work. Some only let party members vote for their party's candidates. Others let all registered voters vote in a primary for either the Democrats or Republicans. When the primary is over, one candidate from each party goes on the ballot for the general election.

5 THE VOTERS DECIDE

Campaigns end on Election Day. Depending on the state and the kind of election, that day is often the first Tuesday in November. Registered voters can vote for whichever candidate they prefer—or none at all.

Bang for the BUCK

$10,000!!

IN 1860, SOME NEW YORK POLITICIANS TRIED TO WIN SUPPORT BY HANDING OUT SANDWICHES.

Some folks say that money makes the world go round—it certainly powers the world of politics. And sometimes the amount spent can make your head spin! Candidates need money to hire staff, place ads, and churn out all those hats and coffee cups with their names on them.

PAC-ING IT IN

There are different ways for candidates to raise money. Sometimes, it comes from groups called political action committees (PACs). PACs support the interests of different groups, like unions that represent workers or businesses. They can give money directly to candidates and their parties. Some PACs are called Super PACs. These committees can't give money directly to a candidate or party or have direct contact with them. But they can pay for ads that support or attack candidates.

CALLING FOR CASH

Another way candidates raise money is by connecting with wealthy people and big businesses that like them and their plans. These donors might expect winners to back laws that help them. But elected officials are not *supposed* to let the donations affect how they vote.

Some states make a certain amount of their funds available to candidates. But if candidates take the money, they have limits on how much money they spend and how much they can collect from donors. Some candidates with lots of their own money don't take the public funds, so they can spend as much as they want on their campaign.

SMALL IS GOOD, TOO

It's not all about donors with big bucks. Candidates can also reach out to individual Americans who don't have a lot of money but who still want to support their campaign. Social media helps connect candidates to these donors. Barack Obama was the first presidential candidate who widely used social media to raise money. Social media also helped him find people to volunteer for him. Some candidates make a big deal about accepting only small amounts of money from American voters. They want to show that the wealthy won't influence their actions.

BY THE NUMBERS

During the election season of 2020, presidential and congressional candidates spent more than $14 billion. Another $2.5 billion was spent on state races.

121

Presidential PRIMARY PICKS

SINCE THE 1920 ELECTION, VOTERS IN NEW HAMPSHIRE HAVE CAST THE FIRST PRIMARY VOTES— SOME TURN OUT AT MIDNIGHT TO PARTICIPATE!

Some people today think money plays too big a role in who gets elected. More than 100 years ago, Americans thought party "bosses," or leaders, had too much power to choose who would even run for office. The leaders sometimes met secretly and made deals to name their preferred candidates. The solution to the problem was primary elections, often called primaries. Primaries are a really big deal when it comes to presidential elections. In primary elections, voters in each state decide which candidates they want to run for president. The candidates who win the most primary elections will become their parties' official nominees.

IN THE RACE

As the election draws near, candidates from both major parties announce they want to be their party's nominee, or choice, for president.

PICK ME!

The candidate then hits the road, trying to convince party members to vote for them in the primaries. These elections are run by the states, so they all work a bit differently. During a presidential election year, primaries usually start in February and run into early summer.

PRIMARY PARTICULARS

In each primary, the number of votes a candidate gets decides how many delegates will go to their party's big convention to vote for them to become the official party nominee for president. A candidate has to collect enough delegates in the primaries to win that honor. In some states, the person who wins the primary gets all the delegates. In others, the delegates are split up according to what percentage of the vote each candidate got.

ON TO THE CONVENTION

Once the primaries are over, the delegates attend the parties' national conventions to formally vote for their candidate. States also have superdelegates—party bigwigs who can vote for whomever they want. Party leaders want to be able to step in if they feel like the nominee is unlikely to win the general election. But superdelegates usually vote for the candidate with the most regular delegates.

A POLITICAL PARTY

Conventions today are more like a celebration than a place to debate. Delegates hear speeches from party leaders and vote to accept the party's platform. They also learn who their nominee will pick as their running mate—the candidate for vice president.

A Big Day

The most famous primary day usually happens in early March, and it's called "Super Tuesday." Because so many states hold their primary elections on that day, there are more delegates awarded than on any other day.

Any Which Way

In the past, before parties held primaries, delegates at national conventions could vote for whichever candidate they wanted, though they often chose the person party leaders wanted. Still, the delegates might have to vote many times to agree on a nominee. In 1924, Democratic delegates voted 103 times before they chose their presidential pick!

RAUCOUS CAUCUS

A handful of states don't have presidential primaries. Instead, they have gatherings called caucuses. Caucuses are conducted by the two parties, not the states, and are typically held at public spots like schools. At these events, supporters of a particular candidate must try to convince other members of their party to back their candidate. Caucus-goers then vote to pick their delegates. (In some cases, they can also vote by mail.) These delegates then choose the people who attend the national convention to vote on a candidate.

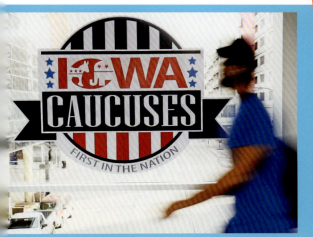

It's DEBATABLE

IN THE 2020 VICE PRESIDENTIAL DEBATE, A FLY SAT ON VICE PRESIDENT MIKE PENCE'S HEAD FOR TWO MINUTES!

Every presidential election since 1960 has featured televised presidential debates. Since 1976, there has also been one for the VP candidates. These debates aim to educate voters about the candidates and the important issues at the time. Today, presidential candidates usually face off three times. One debate focuses on things happening inside the U.S. Another addresses foreign affairs. The third is called a town hall meeting, where average Americans get to ask the candidates questions themselves.

I'm available for parties!

MEMORABLE MOMENTS

Depending on what they say, candidates have been known to score points with voters—or say or do things that hurt their chances. Below are some prime examples.

1980: Ronald Reagan asked viewers, "Are you better off now than you were four years ago?" The economy had worsened under his challenger, President Jimmy Carter. Many viewers answered the question with a big no and voted Reagan into office.

It's been a pleasure defeating you.

1992: In the debate between President George H. W. Bush, Bill Clinton, and third-party candidate Ross Perot, cameras caught Bush looking at his watch. To some viewers, this action made it seem like the president was eager to leave rather than tackle the issues. Bill Clinton went on to win the election.

Rookie mistake.

2012: Republican candidate Mitt Romney argued that President Barack Obama had let the U.S. Navy shrink in size. Obama replied that the military also had fewer "horses and bayonets" than in the past, because the nature of weapons and warfare had changed. Americans were soon doing online searches for the phrase "horses and bayonets," and Barack Obama was ultimately reelected.

THE GREAT DEBATES

For decades, many voters weren't able to see or hear presidential candidates in person. But in 1960, televisions allowed Americans to watch Richard Nixon and John F. Kennedy in the first presidential debates broadcast on the small screen. Nixon was vice president at the time, and Kennedy a senator.

People listening on the radio thought Nixon performed well. But those watching thought Kennedy was the clear winner. He looked strong and healthy, while Nixon, who had recently been in the hospital for a bad knee, looked, well, sick. The candidates held three more debates, giving many Americans their first close-up of Kennedy. He went on to win a very close race for the presidency.

LONG-WINDED

Some of the most memorable political debates took place long before the television or the radio was invented. In 1858, Abraham Lincoln was running for the U.S. Senate against Stephen Douglas, one of two senators from Illinois. The two spoke at seven events across Illinois, talking frequently about slavery—and each often talking for 90 minutes straight! The debates became news around the country, with newspapers printing what each candidate had said. Lincoln lost the race, but the debates made him a rising figure in the new Republican Party. Two years later, he won the presidency.

The Role OF POLLS

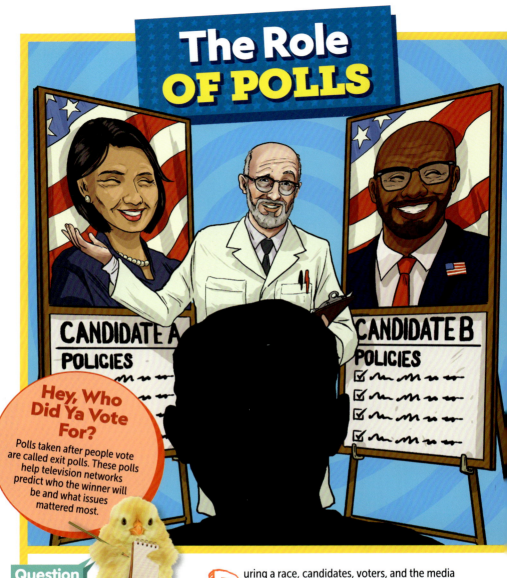

Hey, Who Did Ya Vote For?
Polls taken after people vote are called exit polls. These polls help television networks predict who the winner will be and what issues mattered most.

Question for you!

DURING A TYPICAL POLITICAL RACE, A SINGLE POLLSTER MIGHT QUESTION ABOUT 1,000 VOTERS.

During a race, candidates, voters, and the media want to know one thing: Who has the best shot at winning? No one can predict the future with total accuracy, of course, but one effective way to measure the mood of voters is by asking them questions. Who do they favor? What issues are important to them? Will they vote at all?

This process of asking questions and recording the results is called opinion polling. The first political polls were done during the 1824 presidential election. But it took until the 1930s for pollsters—the people who conduct polls—to come up with scientific tools that made polls more accurate. Still, even today, polls can't always measure exactly what voters think or what they will do.

ASKING AROUND

Polls are conducted by media companies, universities, non-profit groups, and private companies working for candidates. Pollsters can't ask every voter what they think, since there are far too many people living in the country. Instead, they take random samples, meaning they talk to a smaller group of people who represent the larger population of voters. "Random" means a voter in Nebraska has the same chance of being questioned as someone in New York. The sample group also tries to reflect the diversity of the country, so it includes men and women, young and old voters, people of different racial, economic, and ethnic backgrounds, and members of all parties or no parties at all.

Polls are usually done by telephone, though nowadays the internet gives pollsters another way to gather data. Once they have their answers, pollsters figure out what percentage of the people they spoke to feel a certain way. These numbers come with a margin of error, which means the percentage could actually be higher or lower by a few points.

POLLING PITFALLS

A lot of math goes into making polls as accurate as possible. But polls aren't perfect! These are some of the problems:

- ★ Questions can sometimes "lead" people to answer a certain way.
- ★ Polls only measure a voter's feelings at one precise moment—and those feelings can change quickly!
- ★ Some people tell pollsters what they think the pollsters want to hear or what most people believe, not their true feelings.
- ★ Supporters of a candidate might refuse to take part in polls, skewing the data.

Tell me what you really think!

NOT ALWAYS ACCURATE

During the 2016 presidential campaign, polls showed Democrat Hillary Clinton with a lead among likely voters. But Republican Donald Trump ended up winning, leading many to wonder, *What happened?* The polls were fairly accurate in measuring the popular vote—in fact, Clinton beat Trump there, as predicted. But polls in a few states with electoral votes that Clinton needed to win were wrong. Lots of people in those states changed their minds right before Election Day—something the polls couldn't predict.

2020 PRESIDENTIAL ELECTION RESULTS
- Democratic-won state
- Republican-won state

Time to VOTE!

I'm gonna run next year!

A Day for Voting

Some people have called for making Election Day a national holiday, to make it easier for people to vote in person. Some states already make the day a state holiday.

After all the primaries, the polls, the conventions, and the campaigning, a political race comes down to Election Day. For most campaigns, that day is the first Tuesday in November. For the federal government, presidents are elected every four years, House members every two years, and one-third of senators every two years as well. These races for Congress shape what a president is able to do while they're in office. It's easier to turn their plans into law when their party controls both chambers of Congress.

VOTING VARIETY

On Election Day, people generally go to the polls, in this case a polling station where people vote. Voting has changed over the centuries. At one time, Americans marked who they favored on pieces of paper called ballots. They placed the ballots in a box, and election officials counted them afterward by hand.

HOW MANY VOTES?

This chart shows the number of popular votes Democratic and Republican presidential candidates received from 2000 to 2020:

YEAR	CANDIDATE	PARTY	POPULAR VOTE	% OF VOTE
2000	George W. Bush* Al Gore	Republican Democratic	50,456,002 50,999,897	47.9 48.4
2004	George W. Bush John Kerry	Republican Democratic	62,028,285 59,028,109	50.7 48.3
2008	Barack Obama John McCain	Democratic Republican	69,456,000 59,934,000	52.9 45.7
2012	Barack Obama Mitt Romney	Democratic Republican	65,446,032 60,589,084	50.9 47.1
2016	Donald Trump* Hillary Clinton	Republican Democratic	62,979,636 65,844,610	46.0 48.1
2020	Joe Biden Donald Trump	Democratic Republican	81,268,924 74,216,154	51.3 46.9

*Lost popular vote but won electoral vote

Today, things have changed. Some voters still mark their choices on paper, but they're counted by a computer. And not everyone has to vote on the same day. Many states let people vote before Election Day, using a variety of methods. This is called early voting.

VOTE FROM ANYWHERE

People can also vote by mail. In the past, voters who knew they were going to be away from home on Election Day could ask for a mail-in ballot. That included people in the military. Today, some states let anyone request a mail-in ballot. As of 2022, eight states conduct their elections primarily via mail.

DUE TO THE COVID-19 PANDEMIC DURING THE 2020 PRESIDENTIAL ELECTION, A WHOPPING **46 PERCENT** OF VOTERS USED MAIL-IN BALLOTS!

It's an HONOR

PRESIDENT JOE BIDEN PRESENTS THE MEDAL OF FREEDOM TO GYMNAST SIMONE BILES.

Words of Wisdom

"The Medal of Freedom represents the reverence the American people have for liberty, and it honors the men and women who through their lives do greatest honor to that freedom."
—President Ronald Reagan

BY THE NUMBERS

The number of Medal of Honor recipients broken up by branch of the U.S. armed forces:

Army soldiers: 2,452
Navy sailors: 749
Marines: 300
Air Force members: 19
Coast Guard members: 1

Along with all its other duties, the federal government takes time to honor Americans for the good things they do for the country. The president, Congress, and the military all give medals for a number of reasons. Here are the country's top honors.

THE MEDAL OF HONOR

Someone's mettle is their ability to survive tough times. The most important military medal for mettle is given by Congress. The Medal of Honor recognizes service members who risk their lives, going "above and beyond the call of duty." It was first awarded during the Civil War. Since then, more than 3,500 of these medals have been given, with honorees from all branches of the military.

THE CONGRESSIONAL GOLD MEDAL

This medal honors people for their achievements and contributions to the country. For a time, it only went to members of the military. Today, though, anyone can get the gold.

A Hero for All

Dr. Mary Edwards Walker is the only woman to have won the Medal of Honor. She was a U.S. Army surgeon who treated both Northern and Southern soldiers, as well as civilians, during the Civil War. At times, Walker risked her life during battles to reach the wounded.

Past winners have included artists, athletes, astronauts, inventors, scientists, and donors to good causes. The youngest winner ever was Roland Boucher at 11 years old. He was honored in 1941 after he rescued five schoolmates who had fallen through ice on a lake.

THE PRESIDENTIAL MEDAL OF FREEDOM

U.S. presidents have their own medal to honor American civilians. The Presidential Medal of Freedom, first awarded in 1963, is given to civilians who have done great things in public or private life. The winners include civil rights activist Martin Luther King, Jr., First Lady Nancy Reagan, singer Elvis Presley, athletes Simone Biles and Megan Rapinoe, and several past presidents.

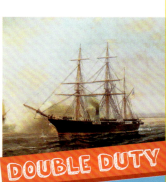

DOUBLE DUTY

There have been 19 service members who have won two Medals of Honor. One of the first was Robert Augustus Sweeney of the U.S. Navy, who was honored in 1881 and 1883. Not once, but twice, Sweeney dived into the water to save fellow sailors who had fallen off their ship. Sweeney is also the only African American to have won the medal twice.

PRESIDENT GEORGE W. BUSH PRESENTS THE MEDAL OF FREEDOM TO BOXER MUHAMMAD ALI.

STATES
of Power

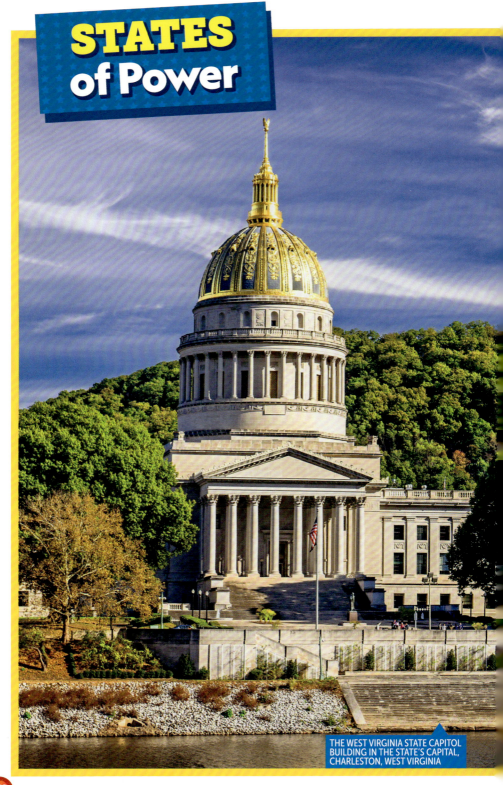

THE WEST VIRGINIA STATE CAPITOL BUILDING IN THE STATE'S CAPITAL, CHARLESTON, WEST VIRGINIA

You've learned a lot about the role of the federal government in the United States. But state governments play a huge role in shaping our lives, too. When the Constitution was written, the 13 states that existed then had almost total control over their own affairs. The Founders tried to balance the idea of "states' rights" while giving the new federal government a greater say in running the country as a whole.

GEORGE MASON, WHO DRAFTED THE VIRGINIA DECLARATION OF RIGHTS

VIRGINIA APPROVED **A DECLARATION** OF RIGHTS IN **1776** THAT SERVED AS A **MODEL** FOR THE **BILL OF RIGHTS** IN THE U.S. **CONSTITUTION.**

But "share and share alike" doesn't always work when it comes to government powers. Finding the right balance between state and federal power is still sometimes a struggle for lawmakers and courts.

WHO DOES WHAT

The Constitution said that federal laws outrank state laws on issues related to the Constitution and federal powers. But some states wanted to put a limit on the federal government. That's what the 10th Amendment was designed to do. It says the federal government only has the power to do the things spelled out in the Constitution. All other powers remain with the states and the people.

Ever since the amendment was passed, courts have ruled on what states can do, and the federal government can't stop them. These powers include making laws on marriage and divorce and on how companies do their business within a state. Supporters of states' rights believe that state governments have a better sense of what their residents want than lawmakers in D.C. do.

A FAMILIAR LOOK

Though states and the federal government sometimes squabble, the two are almost mirror images of each other. Every state has a constitution built on the ideas of separation of powers and checks and balances. State governments have legislative, executive, and judicial branches as well. And every state except Nebraska has a bicameral legislature, which, you might remember, means it has two chambers. As with the federal Constitution, states can amend their constitutions, too.

States carry out elections, and Democrats and Republicans are the two major parties in every state. Voters in some states, though, have elected governors or lawmakers who are independent or members of third parties.

Not so fast!

WHEN STATES DISAGREE

At different times in U.S. history, Congress passed laws that lawmakers from some states didn't like. One of those lawmakers was John C. Calhoun of South Carolina. While serving as vice president in the 1820s, he wrote that states could nullify, or veto, laws they thought were unconstitutional. President Andrew Jackson disagreed. When South Carolina wanted to nullify a tax law, he was ready to send troops to stop them. Since then, Arkansas has also attempted to nullify a federal law, but its case was rejected by the Supreme Court.

133

Go, GOV, Go!

SAM HOUSTON HAS A CLAIM TO FAME—HE'S THE ONLY PERSON TO SERVE AS GOVERNOR IN TWO STATES, TENNESSEE AND TEXAS.

Every state's executive branch is headed by a governor elected by voters. Like the president, governors can sign bills into law or veto them. They also carry out the laws, as the president does, and in some states they appoint judges and other government officials.

Laws vary on how long a governor can serve. In 28 states, governors are limited to two consecutive terms. In eight states, governors are limited to two terms in their lifetime. Other states allow them to hold office for as long as voters choose them. Most governors serve four-year terms, except in New Hampshire and Vermont, where the term is two years. Some states have age requirements or only allow people who have lived there a certain number of years to run for governor. Other states don't have those limits. Oregon has one oddity the other states don't—its governor can't be impeached. But they can be recalled by a popular vote.

EXECUTIVE ASSISTANCE

A governor can't handle all the executive duties alone. The state's executive branch has other officials to help them with their jobs. Some officials are found in every state, such as the attorney general and insurance commissioner. Depending on the state, these officials may be elected, chosen by the governor and approved by the legislature, or appointed by the state legislature or a supreme court. Some of these positions are named in the state constitution, and some were created by the legislature.

The state executive branch also has various departments. Its leaders are similar to a president's Cabinet. They advise the governor and help carry out their policies.

EXECUTIVE OFFICERS ACROSS THE COUNTRY

Along with a governor, attorney general, and insurance commissioner, all states have an agriculture commissioner, a labor commissioner, a public service commissioner, and a superintendent of schools. Some states also have the following jobs:

★ 45 states have a lieutenant governor (basically a vice governor).

★ 47 states have a secretary of state (monitors state records and elections).

★ 19 states have a comptroller (helps watch over a state's money).

★ 48 states have a treasurer (in charge of the state's money).

★ 47 states have an auditor(s) (reviews how the state and local government spend their money).

★ 49 states have a natural resources commissioner (protects and manages public lands, water, and natural resources).

THE SUN SETS OVER TUNNEL VIEW IN CALIFORNIA'S YOSEMITE NATIONAL PARK.

No Doubt About It
Ronald Reagan's 1984 win is what's called a landslide—when one candidate beats another by a huge amount.

Nailed it!

MOVIN' ON UP

Being elected governor can be good on-the-job training for those seeking the highest office—POTUS. Starting with Thomas Jefferson, 17 presidents served as governor before moving into the Oval Office. One of the most successful was Ronald Reagan. He had no political experience when he was elected governor of California in 1966. But voters certainly knew who he was—he had appeared in dozens of movies and TV shows before running for office. California voters liked how he handled the state's finances, and they voted him back as governor in 1970. A decade later, running as a Republican, Reagan defeated incumbent president Jimmy Carter. Reagan survived an assassination attempt in 1981 and called for cutting taxes and strengthening the military. He was reelected in 1984 with 525 electoral votes—the most ever.

Laying Down THE LAWS

THE IDAHO STATE HOUSE OF REPRESENTATIVES IN SESSION, MAKING ARGUMENTS FOR AND AGAINST A BILL

Words of Wisdom

"It's appropriate to celebrate public service, and the thoughtful people who choose to serve. They symbolize what is good and decent about this historic citizen legislature."
—Robert L. Ehrlich, Jr., former governor of Maryland

To make laws, each state has a sort of mini Congress. All states except Nebraska have a legislature with a senate and a larger body that is similar to the U.S. House of Representatives (Nebraska has only one group of legislators, called senators). Most states call their legislature a general assembly, but Massachusetts and New Hampshire call it a general court. States also have different names for the larger chamber: While most call it a house of representatives, some call it a state assembly or a house of delegates. Most members of the lower chamber serve two-year terms, and senators usually serve for four years.

I'm one of a kind!

Nebraska Legislative Districts

BY THE NUMBERS

New Hampshire has the largest house of representatives in the country, with 400 members—in a state with fewer than 1.4 million people! Alaska has the fewest representatives, with 40.

136

BILL THRILLS

No matter what they're called, state legislatures serve the same function as Congress. They write bills that become the basis of new laws in their states. Bills can usually be introduced in either chamber, except for those related to taxes, which in some places must come from the lower chamber. Then bills go through committees before the entire chamber votes on them. Same as in Congress, bills must be approved by both chambers—except in Nebraska, of course. Then they are sent to the governor.

In some states, governors can play another role in the lawmaking process. When the legislature isn't meeting, the governor can call senators and representatives back to the state capital for a special session. These sessions are usually focused on just one or two issues and might concentrate on an emergency. The rest of the states let either the governor or the lawmakers themselves call a special session.

Sorry, folks!

PAY FOR STATE **LAWMAKERS** VARIES, BUT IN **NEW MEXICO,** MEMBERS AREN'T **PAID** AT ALL!

A DAY AT THE OFFICE

Senators and representatives can be lawyers or farmers, business owners or teachers, or they can be retired. Serving as a legislator is a part-time position in most states, so most lawmakers need to keep their day jobs! Only 10 states have full-time legislatures, though members don't meet every month of the year. In almost all states, lawmakers need to be fast workers—most legislative sessions last just a few months, or sometimes only four weeks. In a handful of states, legislators only meet every other year.

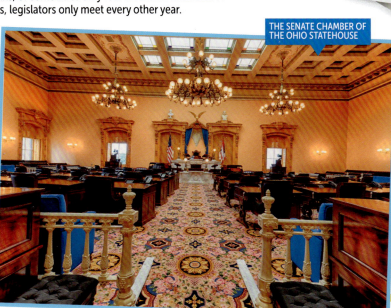

THE SENATE CHAMBER OF THE OHIO STATEHOUSE

137

Judging THE STATES

A JUDGE AT WORK

BECOMING A JUDGE

Judges are
- ☐ appointed by the governor, with approval from the legislature;
- ☐ chosen by the governor from among several candidates recommended by a special committee;
- ☐ elected by voters;
- ☐ appointed by the governor for a set term (in some states, after appointed judges finish their term, they have to win an election to keep their seat); or
- ☐ appointed by the legislature.

Just like in Washington, D.C., the third branch in state governments is the judicial branch. State constitutions usually call for a supreme court, also known as a court of last resort. That court decides if a law or executive order violates a state's constitution. Once the court makes a decision, the case is settled, with one major exception: If a case involves an aspect of federal law or if it relates to the U.S. Constitution, it can be appealed to the U.S. Supreme Court. SCOTUS, though, does not have to accept all these appeals.

STATE COURTS OF ALL SORTS

States have lower courts that mirror the federal system. These trial courts go by different names, but they handle both criminal and civil cases. There is typically another layer of appellate courts between the trial courts and the court of last resort.

States also have courts set up to hear only specific kinds of cases:

★ **PROBATE COURTS** When there's no will, there's still a way to divide up an estate. This is one of the main duties of probate courts, which address legal issues when someone dies without a will. These courts may also decide if a sick person can no longer make decisions or pay bills and needs someone to do it for them.

★ **FAMILY COURTS** Some laws deal with the relationships between family members. Family courts hear cases involving such things as divorce and custody.

★ **JUVENILE COURTS** Not all lawbreakers are adults. States have a separate court system for people under 18 who break the law. (In some cases, though, a court might rule that a teen should be tried as an adult.) The goal of the juvenile court system is to help youths with problems that led them to commit crimes. With that help, they'll hopefully be less likely to break the law as adults.

Judges serve terms as short as one year or as long as they choose until they reach the age of 70. Rhode Island judges can serve for life. Most states set term limits ranging between six and 10 years.

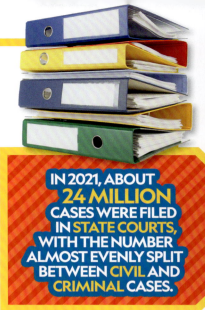

IN 2021, ABOUT **24 MILLION** CASES WERE FILED IN STATE COURTS, WITH THE NUMBER ALMOST EVENLY SPLIT BETWEEN CIVIL AND CRIMINAL CASES.

A LAWYER AT WORK

FROM STATES TO SCOTUS

Many important U.S. Supreme Court cases started in state courts. One such case was *Loving* v. *Virginia* (1967): A Black woman and a white man broke a Virginia law at the time that forbade marriage between people of different races. After they were convicted, they appealed the decision but lost in the Virginia courts. The case eventually went to the Supreme Court, which decided in their favor. As a result, all state laws banning interracial marriage were thrown out.

GREAT DEBATE: SHOULD JUDGES BE ELECTED?

In federal courts, most judges are appointed by the president, and the Senate must then approve them before they take the bench. States, as you've seen, have different ways to select judges, including electing them. But not everyone thinks judges should be elected. Here are a few reasons for and against in the debate.

LET THE VOTERS CHOOSE

Supporters of electing judges argue these points:

★ Voters elect other officials who have a large impact on their lives. They should be able to choose the judges who might hear cases that affect them.

★ Elections give voters the chance to learn about the judicial candidates and decide who would do the best job. Candidates have to convince voters that they have the legal skills to succeed at the job. The campaign process also lets voters see the candidates' different political and judicial views so they can choose the person whose values match theirs and those of their community. Judicial candidates also get to hear the views of the voters.

★ If a judge does something wrong, voters can vote them out of office. Appointed judges can be impeached, but that rarely happens, most likely because the number of votes needed to convict is high.

★ Electing judges helps keep a state's judiciary branch totally independent from the legislative and executive branches.

Words of Wisdom

"One virtue of judicial elections ... is that they expose judges to the real people who fill their jury and witness boxes."

—Martin J. Siegel, former assistant U.S. attorney

Words of Wisdom

"When you enter one of these courtrooms, the last thing you want to worry about is whether the judge is more accountable to a campaign contributor ... than to the law."

—Supreme Court Justice Sandra Day O'Connor

VOTE NO ON JUDICIAL ELECTIONS

Americans who oppose electing judges make these points:

★ Elections for judges, especially for state supreme courts, have become more expensive. As with other elections, some people fear that judicial candidates will favor people or groups that give them the most money. If some judges do that, people will no longer trust that the whole judicial system works fairly.

★ Voters often don't get enough information about judicial candidates to make a good decision. They might end up voting for someone because of their political party, and not because of their legal background.

★ Governors, lawmakers, and nominating committees tend to have more knowledge about judicial candidates and the judicial system than typical voters do.

★ Judges aren't supposed to hear cases in which they have a connection to any of the people involved. But judges might hear a case anyway involving one of their donors and may feel pressure to make the donors happy.

★ A judge might have the next election in mind during a trial, and may make a decision they think most voters want, instead of making a fair legal decision.

OF ALL LEGAL CASES IN THE UNITED STATES, 95 PERCENT ARE FILED IN STATE COURTS.

State DOs and DON'Ts

YOU CAN'T DO THAT

State governments can do a lot, but the U.S. Constitution says there are some things they can't do, such as:

- print paper money or mint coins,
- sign treaties with foreign nations,
- declare war,
- let private ships attack or capture enemy ships,
- give someone a noble title, such as "lord" or "lady," or
- keep an army or build warships during peacetime, unless Congress approves.

tate governments keep busy. Creating and enforcing laws is just one of their duties. Read on to learn about some others.

CREATE LOCAL GOVERNMENTS

The Constitution doesn't say a word about how local government should be created or run, so each state calls the shots. State constitutions spell out how local governments are set up and what powers they have. These local governments can do only what their state constitutions or legislatures say they can do. This idea is based on an 1868 Iowa case presided over by Judge John F. Dillon. His rulings are called Dillon's Rule.

Over time, local governments got tired of always having to ask the state's permission to handle certain issues. Some states decided to give local governments more freedom with something called home rule, meaning local governments can do what they want unless a law or the state or U.S. Constitution specifically says they can't. Today, most states allow home rule; other states have a mixture of Dillon's Rule and home rule.

SET UP SCHOOLS

Because the Constitution didn't mention anything about how kids should be educated, the states have the job of deciding what schools teach. States create local school districts to oversee individual schools and to help fund them. The federal government and local governments pitch in some money, but the states are the ones spending the big bucks—almost half of school funding comes from the states. States also set the standards for the education people need to become teachers.

HELP WITH HEALTH

Along with the federal government, state governments help people get medical insurance through the Affordable Care Act. They also set policies and pass laws promoting healthy lifestyles. States require kids to get vaccines to prevent certain diseases, like the measles, before they can go to school. They can also give money to hospitals and health care providers.

ROLL OUT ROADS

Roads in the United States are a lot like the government—some are federal, some are state, and some are local. State departments of transportation are important in building and maintaining roads. They usually focus on highways, though some money also goes to local roads. Part of the funds that keep roads in good shape comes from taxes that drivers pay when they gas up their cars.

BY THE NUMBERS

In 2019, the 50 states spent more than $125 billion on roads.

143

THEY CAN DO WHAT?

Me, follow orders? That's cute.

You've learned that constitutions spell out a lot of what state governments and the federal government can and can't do. Other government powers come from court decisions. Here are some things governments can do that you might not know about.

TRY TO TRAIN CATS

Not all governments would take on this task. But the CIA did in the 1960s in a project called Acoustic Kitty. The agency thought cats would make perfect spies, as no one would suspect them. The idea was to implant a tiny microphone and recorder inside a cat and have it stroll around where enemies hung out. The cat would pick up what the enemies said, then head back to the agency. The CIA learned what most people already know—cats are not easy to train! The CIA spent millions on this project, which was soon scratched.

SPEND MONEY ON BIZARRE THINGS

In recent years, one California university got three million dollars from the feds to research some video games, to see if players developed skills that would be useful to businesses. Other government money has gone to maintaining buildings that no one was using and to a study that wanted to solve this puzzle: Why do chimps throw their poop?

PUNISH PARENTS IF A KID SKIPS SCHOOL

Not all parents, of course—just Maryland parents or caregivers of kids between the ages of five and 18, if the kids are caught skipping school. Adults can be charged with breaking the law and may have to pay a fine or stay behind bars. They can also choose to do community service instead—like picking up garbage in public places or helping a local nonprofit group.

GO THROUGH YOUR GARBAGE

You might be wondering who would want to wade through your waste. Well, the police might, if they think you're doing something illegal. They need a search warrant to look for evidence inside your house, but once your garbage is out on the street, anyone can poke through it!

TAKE YOUR STUFF— AND NOT PAY

Don't mind if I do!

In all states, police can take a suspect's cars, money, or other valuables if they suspect they were used during alleged criminal activity. These valuables are called assets, and the seizing of them is called asset forfeiture. In some cases, though, the suspects are never actually arrested or convicted, so some lawmakers want to make it harder for police to seize assets.

TAKE PRIVATE PROPERTY

Ah, home, sweet home—until the government decides it wants to build something where you live. Constitutions let governments take someone's property if it's going to be used in a way that benefits everyone, a process called eminent domain. This can include selling the property to businesses that want to build on it. But governments don't get the property for free—they have to pay residents a fair price for the land. This happened in Massachusetts, for example, when the state took some property from a private company to build a new road.

145

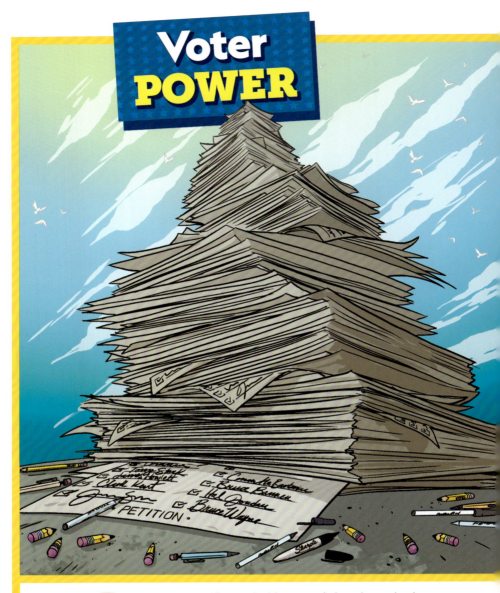

Voter POWER

(Almost) Payday

To try to get more people to vote, Arizonans considered a ballot measure to award a million dollars to a random voter each election. The lure of big bucks wasn't enough—the measure failed.

State legislators aren't the only people who can propose laws. In some states, voters can take charge or at least have a say in making laws and changes to a constitution. They can even give the heave-ho to some elected officials who aren't up to the job.

VOTERS SAY YEA OR NAY

Voters can help make laws in several ways. One is called a referendum. This process starts in the legislature: Lawmakers pass a proposed law or constitutional amendment. Then it's placed on the ballot so voters can choose to accept or reject it.

TAKING THE INITIATIVE

Voters play an even bigger role with initiatives. These votes let ordinary people themselves propose a new law or amendment. In some states, initiatives are called propositions or ballot measures. South Dakota was the first state to let voters initiate laws. Now, 24 states have initiatives. In New Mexico and Maryland, voters can't propose laws, but they can vote to overturn them.

The initiative ball gets rolling when the people who support it go out and collect signatures. They ask registered voters to sign a paper called a petition. The petition spells out the proposed proposition, and a person's signature shows that they support putting it on the ballot. The number of signatures needed varies from state to state. If a measure makes the ballot, voters can vote for or against it.

TO STAY OR GO?

Voters in most states can launch initiatives to try to remove someone from office. This is called a recall, and anyone from governors to members of a local board of education could face one. Unlike an impeachment, a recall initiative might target an official who hasn't done anything wrong. Voters might decide they just don't like the person!

The recall process is similar to the one used for an initiative. People must collect signatures to put a recall vote on the ballot. Voters might start hundreds of recall efforts a year, but usually only a small number reach the ballot. If a recall vote does happen, voters might have to answer a simple question: Should the person be kept in office? In some states, voters can also choose who would replace the official facing a recall.

YUP, PEOPLE VOTED FOR THAT

Initiatives and referendums might deal with topics that seem a little strange. Here are a few that made the ballot:

★ San Francisco voters gave the thumbs-up to an initiative that let a local police officer patrol the streets while carrying a ventriloquist's dummy—a doll with a mouth that moves and can appear to talk.

★ In the small town of Castlewood, Virginia, voters decided they didn't want to be a town anymore. They voted to get rid of the charter that made them a town and let the county take over the government.

★ In 2010, some residents of Denver wanted to be ready if aliens ever landed there. They supported an initiative to create an "extraterrestrial affairs commission" to handle any close encounters with visitors from outer space. Denver voters, however, turned down the idea.

TO CHANGE THE CONSTITUTION IN CALIFORNIA, PEOPLE BACKING AN INITIATIVE MUST COLLECT ALMOST ONE MILLION SIGNATURES.

Whoa, that's a lot!

'Sup!

147

STATE CAPITAL IDEAS

Each state has a capital city—with a capitol building where lawmakers meet. Here are some captivating capital and capitol facts!

BOSTON, MASSACHUSETTS

This capital of Massachusetts claims some historical firsts. It was the first city in the country to have a public park (Boston Common), a public school (Boston Latin), and a post office. Baseball fans may already know that Boston was the site of the first World Series game in 1903. And this is sweet—the city also had the first chocolate factory, which opened in 1765.

BATON ROUGE, LOUISIANA

If you want to see all of Louisiana's capitol in Baton Rouge, look up, and up, and up. At a height of 450 feet (137 m), it's the tallest capitol in the country. To build it, a local railway company constructed a special set of tracks that went right to the site. Trains hauled 2,500 railcars filled with building materials, such as bricks, marble, bronze, stone, and sand.

SANTA FE, NEW MEXICO

No one can ever put you in a corner in New Mexico's capitol. The building in Santa Fe is the only round capitol in the country, and it's known, not surprisingly, as the Roundhouse. Santa Fe is also home to the oldest capitol building in the country. The Spanish built the Palace of the Governors as a capitol in 1610 when they ruled New Mexico.

MORE CAPITAL FACTS

★ Four state capitals are named for presidents: Jackson, Mississippi; Jefferson City, Missouri; Lincoln, Nebraska; and Madison, Wisconsin.

★ Phoenix is the largest capital by population, with about 1.7 million people. The smallest capital is Montpelier, Vermont, with around 8,000 people.

★ Honolulu, Hawaii, and Austin, Texas, once served as national capitals—both Hawaii and Texas were independent countries before becoming part of the United States.

DES MOINES, IOWA

The capital of Iowa is Des Moines. But it might have been called Fort Raccoon, if Captain James Allen had gotten his way. The city was built where the Des Moines and Raccoon Rivers meet. Allen wanted to build a fort there named for the masked mammal, but the U.S. government chose to call it Fort Des Moines instead.

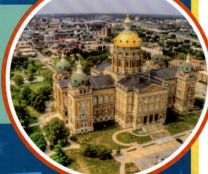

ANNAPOLIS, MARYLAND

Annapolis is Maryland's capital and the home of the State House, the oldest state capitol still in use. Construction for the building began in 1772, and, for a brief time after the American Revolution, it served as the U.S. Capitol. Topping the State House is the oldest wooden dome in the country—and not one nail was used to build it! Wooden pegs and iron straps hold it all together.

Count On COUNTIES

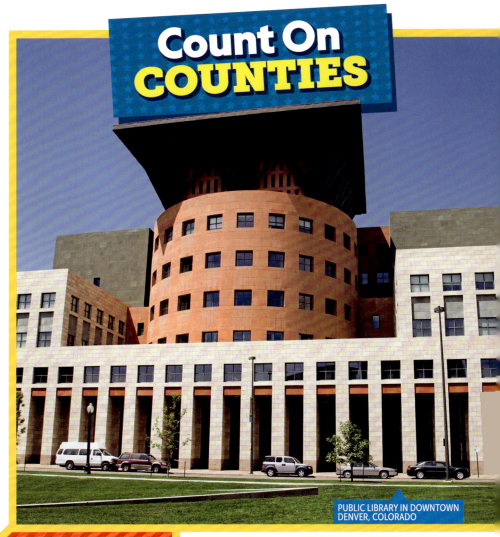

PUBLIC LIBRARY IN DOWNTOWN DENVER, COLORADO

MORE THAN HALF OF ALL AMERICANS LIVE IN ABOUT 5 PERCENT OF THE COUNTRY'S COUNTIES.

All but two states (Connecticut and Rhode Island) have another layer of government called counties wherein people can have a say. (Those two states *do* have counties, but not elected county officials.) Not all states call their counties "counties." Alaska has boroughs, and Louisiana has parishes. No matter what they're called, counties help state governments carry out important duties.

KEEPING THE COUNTIES RUNNING

Counties came to America from England, where they were first called shires. The first county in colonial America was created in Virginia in 1634. Today, state laws and constitutions spell out the powers counties have. Some have home rule and so have greater freedom to run their own affairs.

Counties encompass towns and cities, along with places that are unincorporated. This means they don't have local officials and rely strictly on the counties for their government services. Counties have their own mini capitals called county seats. Most government offices are located there, and a large county might have two towns that serve as seats.

COUNTY DUTIES

Many counties tackle some of the same issues states do. A county's responsibilities can include

- providing education, roads and bridges, and medical care;
- enforcing laws through sheriff departments and running courts;
- paying for libraries, parks, and other public services;
- collecting taxes on property; and
- running special agencies to help military veterans.

One key person in county government is the clerk, who keeps track of important records, such as births, deaths, marriages, and property sales.

Not that kind of seat!

BY THE NUMBERS

- Number of U.S. counties: 3,142
- Largest county by population: Los Angeles, California, with more than 10 million people
- Smallest county by population: Kalawao, Hawaii, with fewer than 100 people
- State with the most counties: Texas, 254
- State with the fewest counties: Delaware, 3

CRITTER CONTROL

Many counties have animal control officers, who are tasked with finding lost pets and dealing with wildlife. And sometimes, these officers get called out on some unusual cases. In Hampton, Virginia, officers were called out to rescue three puppies that turned out to not be puppies at all—they were baby raccoons. In Florida, officers picked up an escaped pet donkey named Romeo that was just walking along the road. And then there was the Arlington, Virginia, resident who discovered an anaconda in her toilet! Animal control officials were able to safely remove the snake and find a snake specialist to care for it.

Please, don't flush.

151

Local MOTION

LET'S MEET

In colonial New England, people took government so seriously that they fined people who didn't show up to town meetings. The meetings were direct democracy in action—people debated and voted on how the town should be run. Only men who paid taxes, though, could vote. In smaller towns, meetings were held every week or month, but over time they became a yearly event. Some New England towns still hold these meetings, which typically focus on how to spend the town's money and passing local laws, but now they don't fine people who don't show.

Show up or pay up!

Whether you live in a tiny town or a sprawling city, your life is touched by local government. These governments are sometimes called municipal governments and are created by the state to carry out duties that are similar to counties'. However, state laws may give more responsibilities to municipalities than counties.

Like states and counties, cities and towns have elected officials who pass local laws, and some form of executive who carries them out. As with counties, the executive may be elected and is usually known as the mayor. This person could also be hired by the legislative body, in which case they are known as a city manager or town manager.

THAT'S SO SPECIAL

Many municipalities have another layer of government within them called special districts, and they usually focus on providing one specific service. This could be paying for the local library, running hospitals, taking care of sewers, or fighting fires. Special districts are created by the states and are usually overseen by boards, commissions, or

SAN FRANCISCO'S ACTING MAYOR, LONDON BREED, ADDRESSES A COMMUNITY MEETING IN 2018.

IN 2021, THE TOWN OF **MONOWI, NEBRASKA**, WAS A ONE-WOMAN SHOW: **ELSIE EILER** WAS THE **MAYOR**, THE TOWN **CLERK**, AND THE **ONLY RESIDENT!**

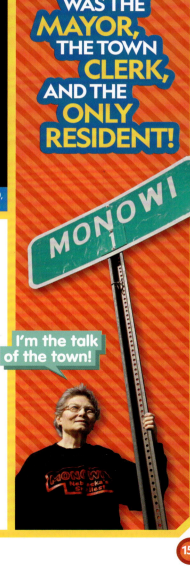

I'm the talk of the town!

authorities. The districts often collect taxes from local residents to pay for these services. Members may be elected or appointed, and can hold other government positions. Some states have more than 2,000 special districts.

RULES FOR SCHOOLS

One kind of district is a school district. Most states have independent school districts, meaning they are separate from the municipal or state government. The districts are run by school boards, whose members are usually elected. Board members set up policies for local schools and hire someone to run their day-to-day operations. Across the country, local governments and independent school boards deal with a lot of cash—in 2019 alone, they spent more than $342 billion on education.

WHATTA JOB!

Mayors and commission members help keep cities and counties running smoothly. But some local government positions aren't quite as well known. Here are a few.

ON THE FENCE

Only a few states have passed laws calling for local towns to have fence viewers, who do a lot more than just look at fences. These fence folks make sure fences that divide properties are in good shape. They also help settle arguments between neighbors if someone builds a fence on another person's property. Fence viewers were more important several hundred years ago, when many people raised animals on their land and fences kept cows and other critters from straying.

Sorry!

QUITE A BUZZ

Mosquitoes are pesky pests, and they can also carry diseases that can make people very sick. Some towns and states have mosquito control boards that try to swat the little suckers before they do damage. One important task for the board is draining pools of water where mosquitoes lay their eggs, before they hatch even more mosquitoes. In some towns, these board members run for office, and in others they are appointed.

WHEN **ZEB TOWNE** RAN FOR REELECTION IN **2014** AS THE LOCAL **DOGCATCHER** IN DUXBURY, VERMONT, ONLY **ONE PERSON** VOTED AGAINST HIM— **HIS WIFE!** SHE DIDN'T LIKE THAT HE HAD TO **CHASE DOWN** DOGS LATE AT **NIGHT.**

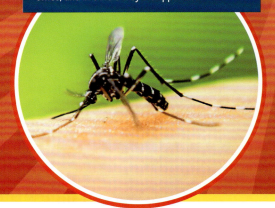

154

FIDO FOR PRESIDENT

It probably doesn't need to be said that animals can't be president or hold any other political office. But that hasn't stopped some pet owners from trying to get their precious pup or cute kitty on the ballot. And in some places, voters and local leaders have made animals honorary members of the government. Let's bone up on animals in politics.

TOP DOG

Dogs can make good mayors, too, as Parker the Snow Dog proved in 2020. Parker was already a popular pooch in Georgetown, Colorado, when local officials named him to the honorary position. He served as a mascot at a local ski area and is something of a canine celebrity, appearing during televised football games in Denver.

Free catnip for all!

THE CAT'S MEOW

Voting for mayor in Omena, Michigan, can be a real zoo—especially when 18 animals are up for the job. That was the case in 2018, when a cat named Sweet Tart won the honorary title, beating out many dogs, another cat, a goat, and a peacock. The town has chosen an animal as its honorary mayor since 2009. Voters pay one dollar to cast a ballot, and the money goes to a local charity.

FROM THE DOG HOUSE TO THE WHITE HOUSE

Honorary mayor is a fine role indeed, but what if a canine has bigger dreams? Satchel, a bull terrier from Tennessee, started a campaign online to run for president. He began his own "Bully Party," with the help of his human campaign manager, Wayne North. When he was out meeting voters, Satchel usually wore an American flag tied around his neck, proving he was one patriotic pup. Since he wasn't officially on the ballot, Satchel had to campaign for write-in votes. There's no record of any voters adding his name to the ballot.

156

GET YOUR GOAT

And have it run for mayor. You can do so if you live in Fair Haven, Vermont. Elsa the goat joined the pet political parade in 2022, when she beat out several other animals to become the town's honorary mayor. Elsa was a baby goat, also called a kid, so it was only fair of Fair Haven to let the town's kids vote for her, too. Elsa followed two other goats that had held the top job, but one of them could have used some training—potty training, that is. It pooped on the town hall floor after being sworn in!

PRESIDENTIAL PREDICTIONS

Not all animals want to run for office, but some still care about politics. During presidential races, some might try to predict who will win. One of these critter predictors was Amelia the flying squirrel. She impressed folks when she said Donald Trump would win in 2016. To make her choice for that election, Amelia picked a pumpkin seed with a *T* on it for Trump over one with a *C* for Hillary Clinton. But Amelia's record snapped in 2020, when she once again went for a seed with *T* for Trump over the one with a *B* for Joe Biden. The incumbent president lost to Biden by 74 electoral votes.

AMELIA THE SQUIRREL DID MORE THAN PREDICT PRESIDENTIAL RACES. SHE ALSO NAMED FOUR DIFFERENT SUPER BOWL WINNERS!

Go, team!

OFFICIALLY ODD

State lawmakers love to choose things to officially represent their state. State flowers and animals are pretty common, but some states have chosen symbols that are a little different. Take a look!

KANSAS HAS AN **OFFICIAL FLYING FOSSIL**, THE REMAINS OF A WINGED REPTILE CALLED A **PTERANODON**. IT HAD A **WINGSPAN** OF ABOUT **24 FEET (7 M)**!

WOOD YOU BELIEVE, **OREGON** HAS A **STATE CHAIN-SAW-CARVING CAPITAL**? IT'S **REEDSPORT**, THE SITE OF AN ANNUAL CHAIN-SAW-CARVING CONTEST.

HERE'S THE POINT— **MARYLAND** NAMED THE CENTURIES-OLD CONTEST OF **JOUSTING** ITS OFFICIAL SPORT.

I'm as surprised as you!

THERE OUGHTTA BE A LAW

And in some cases, there is a law, even if it's weird or wacky. Here are some state and local laws that were once on the books or are still in force today.

Why only Sunday??

SUNDAY SHOULD BE A DAY OF REST FOR HUNTERS **IN VIRGINIA.** THE STATE SAYS THEY **CAN'T TAKE A SHOT AT ANY BIRD OR WILD ANIMAL** ON THAT DAY NEAR A PLACE OF WORSHIP. IT'S ALSO ILLEGAL ANYTIME TO TRY TO KILL OR CAPTURE A WILD CRITTER **NEAR A FOREST FIRE.**

IN PARTS OF RENO, NEVADA, YOU HAVE TO **KEEP WALKING;** IT'S ILLEGAL TO SIT ON A PUBLIC SIDEWALK, EVEN IF IT'S ON A BLANKET OR A CHAIR.

WE DIDN'T SEE THIS COMING: PEOPLE IN YAMHILL, OREGON, HAVE TO LEAVE TOWN IF THEY WANT TO TRY TO LEARN ABOUT THEIR FUTURE. PALM READING, ASTROLOGY, AND OTHER SIMILAR PRACTICES USED TO SEE INTO THE FUTURE ARE OUTLAWED THERE.

I see ... handcuffs?

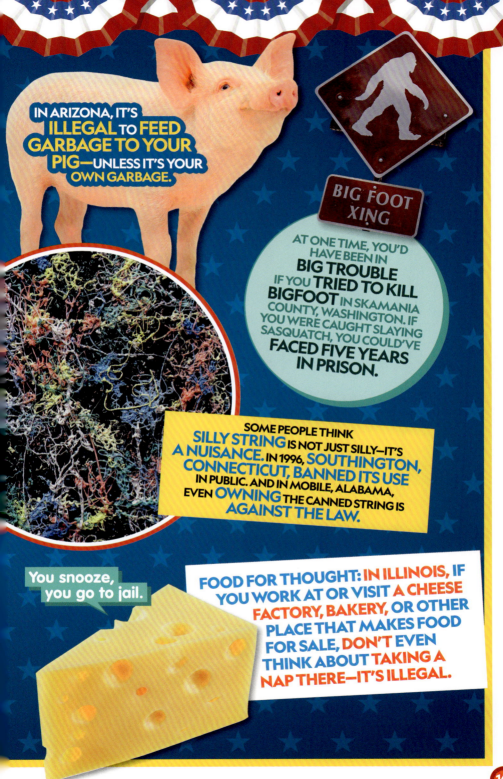

IN ARIZONA, IT'S **ILLEGAL** TO **FEED GARBAGE TO YOUR PIG**—UNLESS IT'S YOUR OWN GARBAGE.

AT ONE TIME, YOU'D HAVE BEEN IN **BIG TROUBLE** IF YOU **TRIED TO KILL BIGFOOT** IN SKAMANIA COUNTY, WASHINGTON. IF YOU WERE CAUGHT SLAYING SASQUATCH, YOU COULD'VE **FACED FIVE YEARS IN PRISON.**

SOME PEOPLE THINK **SILLY STRING** IS NOT JUST SILLY—IT'S **A NUISANCE.** IN 1996, **SOUTHINGTON, CONNECTICUT, BANNED ITS USE** IN PUBLIC. AND IN MOBILE, ALABAMA, EVEN **OWNING** THE CANNED STRING IS **AGAINST THE LAW.**

You snooze, you go to jail.

FOOD FOR THOUGHT: IN ILLINOIS, IF YOU WORK AT OR VISIT A CHEESE FACTORY, BAKERY, OR OTHER PLACE THAT MAKES FOOD FOR SALE, DON'T EVEN THINK ABOUT TAKING A NAP THERE—IT'S ILLEGAL.

Nations Within A NATION

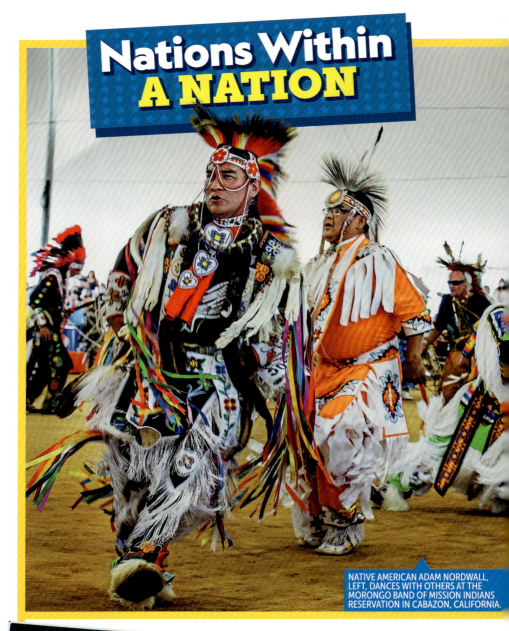

NATIVE AMERICAN ADAM NORDWALL, LEFT, DANCES WITH OTHERS AT THE MORONGO BAND OF MISSION INDIANS RESERVATION IN CABAZON, CALIFORNIA.

The United States is one big nation, but some people may not know that there are hundreds of smaller nations within it—the Native American tribal nations. The U.S. government and some states have recognized almost 600 tribal nations. Being recognized means Native American tribes can set up their own governments and receive funds and services from the U.S. government. It also gives the tribes the power to control their own lands, often known as reservations.

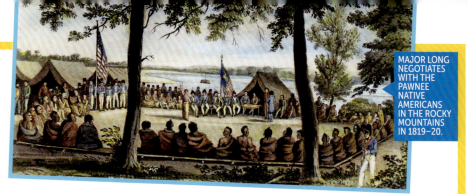

MAJOR LONG NEGOTIATES WITH THE PAWNEE NATIVE AMERICANS IN THE ROCKY MOUNTAINS IN 1819–20.

A LONGING FOR LAND

Europeans arriving on the continent in colonial days noticed that Native Americans were formed into separate tribes, and the colonists treated the tribes as independent nations. The settlers acknowledged this by signing treaties with them. For example, in 1778, a treaty was signed declaring peace between the Americans and the Delaware Nation.

But keeping the peace between various tribes and the white Americans who were moving west wasn't easy. Settlers wanted to take the land where the tribes lived and hunted. Fighting frequently broke out between the two sides. Some tribes chose to sign treaties that gave portions of their land to the United States as long as they could also keep some for themselves.

TREATIES MADE AND BROKEN

In some cases, though, treaties forced the tribes from their traditional lands. That's what happened during the 1830s, when thousands of Cherokee in southeastern states were forced to move into what is now Oklahoma. The brutal conditions they faced on the journey, during which nearly 4,000 Native Americans died, is now known as the Trail of Tears.

Unfortunately, many times, the federal government and individual states simply ignored the treaties they had signed. They didn't make promised payments and often took land belonging to the tribes. In other cases, government officials made treaties with the tribes, but the Senate never ratified them and the tribes were left with nothing.

A FIGHT FOR RIGHTS

In most cases, tribes never regained the land they lost, and their reservations were controlled by the federal government. During the 20th century, tribes tried to gain more control over their own affairs. Congress passed laws that gave the tribes more legal rights, such as running their own schools. One law passed in 1924 finally made Native Americans not only members of their tribes but U.S. citizens as well. For the first time in U.S. history, Native Americans could vote in federal elections, though some states still prevented them from voting in state elections.

Tons of Treaties

Between 1778 and 1871, the U.S. Senate ratified 370 treaties with different tribes.

SCOTUS WEIGHS IN

Several Supreme Court decisions have shaped the relationship between tribal nations and the U.S. government. Here are a few of the big ones:

★ *Worcester* v. *Georgia* (1832): Said that tribal nations were independent states with a right to claim their own lands.

★ *Talton* v. *Mayes* (1896): Upheld the rights of tribes to pass laws and conduct trials between tribal members on tribal lands.

★ *California* v. *Cabazon Band of Mission Indians* (1987): Denied state and county governments the right to regulate gambling on Native American lands, giving tribes a way to make money.

★ *Minnesota* v. *Mille Lacs Band of Chippewa Indians* (1999): Ensured the rights of tribes to hunt and fish on lands they had given to the federal government, as spelled out in treaties.

Governing NATIVE AMERICAN COUNTRY

THE SUN RISES OVER HUNTS MESA IN MONUMENT VALLEY NAVAJO TRIBAL PARK.

Words of Wisdom

"As a sovereign nation preexisting the federal and state governments, we continue to assert our inherent right to make our own laws and have our people and reservation lands be governed by them."

—Oglala Sioux Tribe president Kevin Killer

OGLALA SIOUX TRIBE FLAG

Altogether, the area of land under the control of tribal nations is larger than all but three states. Tribal nations are spread out across the United States, though more than 200 of them are in Alaska alone. Still, this is only a fraction of the land they once controlled. In 1900, tribes owned about 10 percent of all U.S. land. That number is now down to about 2.3 percent, because federal laws took the lands that the government considered extra and gave them to non-Native settlers, many of whom were white.

The largest Native American reservation belongs to the Diné, also known as the Navajo. Their lands cover about 17 million acres (7 million ha) in parts of Arizona, New Mexico, and Utah. The smallest reservation belongs to the Pit River Tribe in California and is just 1.32 acres (0.5 ha). It's the site of a tribal cemetery. The tribe, though, also owns other lands.

FAMILIAR FORMS OF GOVERNMENT

Just as they vary in size, tribal nations are different in how they set up their governments. Many tribes follow a model based on a written constitution provided by the U.S. government. Others follow written and unwritten centuries-old rules that dictate how a tribe should govern itself.

Tribal governments include the following:

★ An elected legislative branch that makes laws, often called a tribal council.

★ An executive branch led by an official who might be called governor, president, chair, or chief. This person might be elected by the council or by the entire voting population.

★ In some tribes, a judicial branch with tribal courts that handle civil cases and some criminal cases.

★ A police force that upholds tribal laws on the reservation. Not all tribes have one.

THE GOVERNMENTS' DUTIES

As with other governments in the United States, tribal nations try to improve the lives of their residents. Some of the issues they address fall in these areas:

- ★ Communications
- ★ Economic growth
- ★ Education
- ★ Environmental problems
- ★ Health care
- ★ Tax collection
- ★ Transportation and roads

Tribal governments often work with federal and state governments to address some of these issues. At the federal level, the Bureau of Indian Affairs, part of the Department of the Interior, works closely with tribal nations. Money from the federal government provides health care and education for many tribal members. Receiving federal money and developing their own businesses are crucial for these nations, as they face higher levels of poverty compared with the rest of the country.

A Good Example

During the 1750s, a union of tribes called the Haudenosaunee had an oral constitution that Benjamin Franklin thought would be a good model for English settlers. Historians have seen one similarity between the Haudenosaunee constitution and the U.S. Constitution: Both call for sharing powers between individual tribes—and states—with a central government.

GIVING BACK

Native Americans have often answered the call to serve the United States during wartime. In the 20th century alone, more than 100,000 Native Americans fought in the country's major wars. During World War II, more than 10 percent of the entire Native American population served in the military. For the Vietnam War, most of the 42,000 Native Americans who served were volunteers.

A CONGRESSIONAL GOLD MEDAL THAT HONORS NATIVE AMERICANS WHO SERVED AS CODE TALKERS IN WWI AND WWII

165

ISLAND LANDS

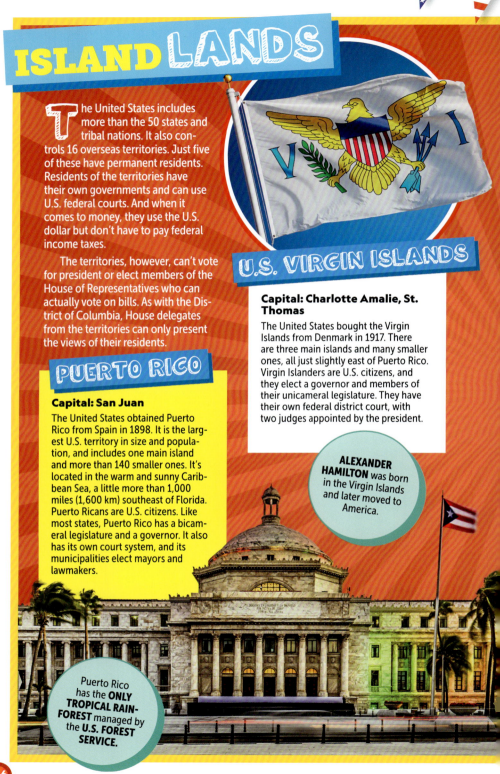

The United States includes more than the 50 states and tribal nations. It also controls 16 overseas territories. Just five of these have permanent residents. Residents of the territories have their own governments and can use U.S. federal courts. And when it comes to money, they use the U.S. dollar but don't have to pay federal income taxes.

The territories, however, can't vote for president or elect members of the House of Representatives who can actually vote on bills. As with the District of Columbia, House delegates from the territories can only present the views of their residents.

U.S. VIRGIN ISLANDS

Capital: Charlotte Amalie, St. Thomas

The United States bought the Virgin Islands from Denmark in 1917. There are three main islands and many smaller ones, all just slightly east of Puerto Rico. Virgin Islanders are U.S. citizens, and they elect a governor and members of their unicameral legislature. They have their own federal district court, with two judges appointed by the president.

PUERTO RICO

Capital: San Juan

The United States obtained Puerto Rico from Spain in 1898. It is the largest U.S. territory in size and population, and includes one main island and more than 140 smaller ones. It's located in the warm and sunny Caribbean Sea, a little more than 1,000 miles (1,600 km) southeast of Florida. Puerto Ricans are U.S. citizens. Like most states, Puerto Rico has a bicameral legislature and a governor. It also has its own court system, and its municipalities elect mayors and lawmakers.

ALEXANDER HAMILTON was born in the Virgin Islands and later moved to America.

Puerto Rico has the **ONLY TROPICAL RAINFOREST** managed by the **U.S. FOREST SERVICE**.

166

AMERICAN SAMOA

Capital: Pago Pago, Tutuila Island

The United States acquired American Samoa in 1899 in a treaty agreement with Germany and Great Britain. It's located in the Pacific Ocean, about halfway between Hawaii and New Zealand, and is made up of five islands and two coral reefs. Residents are called American nationals, not citizens. Samoan Americans can freely enter and live in the United States, if they choose. American Samoa has a bicameral legislature, meaning it has two chambers, and a governor. Its high court judges are chosen by the U.S. secretary of the interior.

NORTHERN MARIANA ISLANDS

Capital: Saipan Island

The Northern Mariana Islands became a U.S. territory in 1975. This commonwealth includes more than a dozen islands and islets located just north of Guam. Its people are U.S. citizens, and most live on Saipan. The government of the territory has a bicameral legislature and a governor, and it also has a federal district court. From 1947 to 1994, the United States ran the Northern Marianas and nearby islands for the United Nations.

American Samoa **HAS TALENT!** It has sent **HUNDREDS OF FOOTBALL PLAYERS** to the United States to play at colleges and in the National Football League.

GUAM

Capital: Hagåtña

The United States acquired Guam from Spain in 1898. It's about 4,000 miles (6,400 km) west of Hawaii, and is the largest island in a group called Micronesia. Its residents are U.S. citizens. Guam has a legislature with just one chamber, a governor, and a federal district court.

GUAM SITS WEST OF THE INTERNATIONAL DATE LINE, WHICH MAKES IT ONE DAY AHEAD OF THE 50 STATES.

People POWER

PROTESTERS GATHER IN PHILADELPHIA'S LOGAN SQUARE.

Words of Wisdom

"It is citizens—ordinary men and women, determined to forge their own future—who throughout history have sparked all the great change and progress."
—Barack Obama

From Guam to Maine and everywhere in between, the American people are at the heart of the nation's government. Remember—the Constitution starts off with "We the People"! The government officials that voters elect serve them, meaning the people are the boss. And as you've seen, people can play a direct role in passing laws and pulling politicians out of office, through the referendum, initiative, and recall.

The First Amendment gives all Americans important rights that can influence how the government is run. The right to free speech means no government agency can limit what people say about political matters. The right to petition lets Americans go directly to Congress to express their feelings on important issues. They can collect signatures on a petition or send letters or emails. And the right of peaceful assembly means people can gather in public to express their views for or against government actions and policies.

SERVING OTHERS

People shape the government in other ways, too. Many municipalities, counties, and states rely on volunteers to serve on commissions and boards. Some of the most common are citizen advisory boards. They can go by several names, including task forces and committees. They're generally set up by municipalities to research a specific topic and make recommendations to elected officials. Some also help government agencies carry out their duties. Volunteers for advisory boards have to be ready to give up some of their free time to do research and attend meetings. Many also have some experience relating to the topic they are studying.

An advisory board may review topics like some of the following:

- Public libraries
- Issues affecting senior citizens
- Small businesses
- Public transportation
- Environmental issues
- Parks and recreation

MILITARY MATTERS

A very special group of volunteers are the people who choose to serve in the U.S. military or the National Guard (though once they're in, they do get paid!). Members of the different branches of the military defend the country and often serve overseas. But their missions help people in the United States, too. Members of the military might be called on to give aid during natural disasters, such as forest fires and hurricanes. They might also keep order if protests turn violent. Members of the Coast Guard perform search missions at sea, trying to rescue ships in distress.

THE JURY'S IN

Americans play another important role in government by serving on juries. During a criminal or civil court case, members of the jury listen to all the facts presented and then make a decision. In a criminal case, they decide if the accused is guilty or not guilty, and in most cases, all jury members must agree on the decision. In civil cases, a jury decides which side presented the best legal case. In a 12-person civil jury, 10 of the members must agree. To find jurors, courts randomly select registered voters or people who have a driver's license. The lawyers or a judge involved can question potential jurors to make sure they will be fair in deciding the case.

Words of Wisdom

"That in controversies respecting property, and in suits between [people], trial by jury is preferable to any other, and ought to be held sacred."

—Virginia State Constitution

169

Do Your PART!

You Have the Power

Another way to speak up is to attend public government meetings or visit lawmakers. You and your friends can be kid lobbyists! Some middle school students in Colorado visited state senators to convince them to make cats and dogs adopted from shelters the official state pets. Their hard work paid off, and a law was passed in 2013.

So are we state employees?

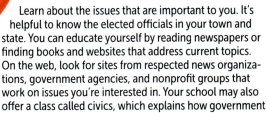

Casting votes and running for elected office is serious business for adults. But that doesn't mean that kids can't play a role in shaping what governments do. Here are some things you can do right now to get involved, or at least after you finish reading this book!

GET INFORMED

Learn about the issues that are important to you. It's helpful to know the elected officials in your town and state. You can educate yourself by reading newspapers or finding books and websites that address current topics. On the web, look for sites from respected news organizations, government agencies, and nonprofit groups that work on issues you're interested in. Your school may also offer a class called civics, which explains how government works and the role citizens play in it.

SPEAK UP

Share your new knowledge with public officials or the public at large. Grab a pen or tap out something on your phone! If you're worried about climate change and have ideas on how to fight it, let your government leaders know. Or share your opinions with the local newspaper. You can write a letter to the editor or an essay for the opinions page.

GIVE YOUR TIME

Politicians and nonprofit groups count on volunteers to get their work done. If there is a candidate you like or a cause you believe in, see how you can help. It could be something as simple as stuffing envelopes or putting up posters. You can also call registered voters to see if they support your candidate.

RAISE MONEY

You've seen how much money it costs to run for government office. You might not have big bucks to give, but in a local race, every little bit helps. You can raise money by holding a bake sale or a car wash. If you want to help a nonprofit, you can ask friends and family to donate to it instead of buying you birthday gifts.

The President Works for You!

Kids can even write to the president. In 2016, eight-year-old Mari Copeny wrote to President Barack Obama about unhealthy water in her hometown of Flint, Michigan. Obama wrote back and then visited the city to learn more about the problem.

SIGN ME UP

When you turn 18, you can vote in state and federal elections. But a lot of people between ages 18 and 29 register to vote, and then never do. One way to get more young people to the polls is to offer preregistration. The idea is that getting people involved in the voting process before they turn 18 will make them more interested in government—and more likely to vote when they hit the legal age. In many states, teens can sign up to vote when they are 16 or 17. In other states, they can preregister if they will turn 18 before the next election.

171

Class ACTS

My platform is no homework!

Young people who want a taste of what it's like to run a campaign and serve others often get their start in school. In a student government, kids learn the basics of the democratic system and the value of playing an active role in their community. Student governments are common in high schools and colleges, but some middle schools have them, too. In younger grades, student governments are often called student councils.

CREATING A COUNCIL

Serving in student government doesn't mean that students set the rules for their schools. But the council does represent the interests of all the students, and it presents ideas to school officials, boards of education, and parents' groups. Student government members work with one or more adult advisers, usually a teacher. In most cases, principals can veto a council's proposal if they think it might harm students or their learning experience.

A student council can take different forms, which is often spelled out in a constitution. In some schools, each homeroom might elect a representative. In other schools, there may be a certain number of representatives for each grade. Or the entire school might elect the officers—usually a president, vice president, treasurer, and secretary—and they serve as the "executive branch" of the government. Then individual grades or classes might elect representatives who act as the "legislative branch." No matter how the government is set up, one thing is always true—students choose the people who will serve on the council.

You're the future of government!

PLENTY TO DO!

Student governments and councils keep busy. If the school doesn't give them money, they have to earn it, usually by having fundraisers. They can also raise money by sponsoring events, such as dances or yard sales. Other duties of student governments include

- ★ promoting school spirit with contests, holiday celebrations, or other events open to all students;
- ★ informing the school of student government activities through newsletters;
- ★ asking students for their ideas on how to make the school better; and
- ★ recruiting students to volunteer in the community or collecting toys, books, or other items for people in need.

STUDENT SENATORS

If you think running a student government is hard, imagine trying to run a nation! That's what some teens do—sort of—every year, as part of Boys and Girls Nations. Two girls from every state and two boys from every state except Hawaii are named "senators" and travel to Washington, D.C. There, in separate sessions for boys and girls, kids pretend they're real senators, proposing and passing bills for the country. They elect a president and vice president, too. While in the nation's capital, the young senators get to meet the actual senators from their state and visit important sites.

Meeting the Bigwigs

Some government officials who attended Boys Nation or Girls Nation include President Bill Clinton, former New Jersey governor Chris Christie, and former Texas governor Ann Richards.

RUNNING FOR REAL

Sure, some young people learn how to govern in school or through Boys and Girls Nations. But some get their political feet wet by actually running for a government office—and winning!

SAIRA BLAIR

Saira Blair was only 18 when she was elected to West Virginia's House of Delegates, making her the youngest person ever to serve in that chamber. A Republican, Blair served from 2014 to 2018. One of the bills she sponsored made cyberbullying a crime, and it was signed into law in 2018.

JEREMY YAMAGUCHI

Jeremy Yamaguchi was no political rookie when he was elected mayor of Placentia, California, in 2011. He was first elected to the city council when he was 19, and served there for three years. At 22, he became the youngest mayor in Placentia history. He had been active in the community, as well, before entering politics; while still in high school, he was named Placentia's Citizen of the Year.

HANNAH ZIMMERMAN

Hannah Zimmerman wouldn't take no for an answer. She was 17 when she won a seat on the New York County Democratic Committee in 2017. She had gotten plenty of people to sign a petition to put her on the ballot. But at the time, New York law said she was too young to run for office, since she was not yet able to vote. Hannah argued her case in front of election officials and was allowed on the ballot. Hannah later founded the Institute for Civic Organizing to get more people involved in politics.

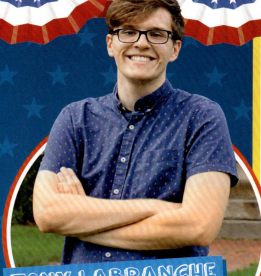

TONY LABRANCHE

Just months after graduating from Souhegan High School in 2020, Tony Labranche was elected to the New Hampshire House of Representatives. Tony said that after surviving cancer when he was 10, he saw how expensive health care could be for many Americans. That sparked his interest in government service, as he hoped to lower medical costs for everyone.

LANDIN STADNYK

When Landin Stadnyk was elected as supervisor for the Scott County Soil and Water Conservation District in 2020, he was the youngest person in the Kentucky government. Actually, at 17, he was the youngest elected official in the whole country! Stadnyk first ran for the job when he was 15. He also served in student government while holding his elected office—and he found time to take some high-level classes, too.

Words of Wisdom

"My message to youth would be, create the world that you want to live in."
—Landin Stadnyk

BENDING THE RULES

The U.S. Constitution says that members of the House of Representatives must be at least 25 years old. But that didn't stop lawmakers from letting someone younger join the House. William Charles Cole Claiborne of Tennessee holds the record as the youngest representative ever. In 1797, at age 22, Claiborne was elected to fill a seat left vacant by Andrew Jackson, the future seventh U.S. president. House members chose to ignore the Constitution and let him serve, and no one seems to have challenged the decision. Claiborne served two terms in the House and was later elected governor of Louisiana and then a U.S. senator for that state.

SYMBOLS OF THE UNITED STATES

Symbols are things that stand for something else. The United States has objects, words, and images that are symbols of the country's government and its values.

Wanna race?

BISON

Millions of bison once roamed all across the United States. They were a major source of food and clothing for many Native American tribes and early white settlers. But during the early 1800s, hunters almost wiped out the bearded beasts. President Theodore Roosevelt helped start the effort to keep bison alive. Today, about 500,000 call the country home. The bison became the national mammal in 2016. And despite its size, the bison is no slowpoke—it can sprint at speeds up to 35 miles an hour (56 km/h)!

THE GREAT SEAL

The official seal is used to show that a president's signature on a document is legit, and it appears on other official papers, too. It's even on the buttons of military uniforms. The U.S. seal is called the Great Seal, and it includes an image of an eagle. In one talon, the eagle holds an olive branch, a symbol of peace. In the other, it holds arrows, which represent war. Americans wanted the world to know that they stood for peace but would fight to protect their freedom. The eagle also holds a banner with the Latin words *E pluribus unum*. This motto means "Out of many, one," reflecting how the 13 original states came together to create one nation. This motto also appears on all U.S. coins in general use today.

U.S. FLAG

The U.S. flag may be the best known symbol of the nation. There are 50 stars, one for each state, and 13 stripes that represent the 13 Colonies at the time of the American Revolution.

UNCLE SAM

Uncle Sam, the bearded bloke with the big hat, is not an official symbol, but Americans have seen him for almost 200 years. The name is thought to come from "Uncle Sam" Wilson, who sold meat to the U.S. government. He stamped barrels of the food with the initials "U.S."—short for the United States. Folks also connected the initials to Uncle Sam himself. The most famous image appeared on posters during World Wars I and II, encouraging Americans to join the military. Uncle Sam is still considered a symbol of patriotism.

OAK TREE

Americans chose the mighty oak as their favorite tree in a national poll in 2001. Three years later, it became the official tree of the United States. Oaks are famous for their strength and long lives, and more than 60 different kinds are found across the country.

THE STAR-SPANGLED BANNER

No professional sporting event would be complete without hearing, "O say can you see ..." Those are the first words of "The Star-Spangled Banner," the country's national anthem. Francis Scott Key wrote the words in 1814, as British troops attacked Baltimore during the War of 1812. Even as enemy fire flew, the U.S. flag kept waving.

BALD EAGLE

The bald eagle is the national bird of the United States. It represents bravery and strength.

I'm kind of a big deal.

TURKEY TAKEOVER

Benjamin Franklin was no fan of the bald eagle. He wrote a letter to his daughter saying that "the turkey is ... a much more respectable bird." Many people came to believe that he wanted the turkey to represent the country, but Franklin's letter was likely said in good fun.

TEST YOUR Knowledge

Every year, hundreds of thousands of people born in foreign countries become United States citizens. But first they have to make the grade by passing a civics and history test. Could you pass the test to become a citizen? Here are some questions based on the ones in the actual test—and you've read the answers somewhere in this book. See how you do, and maybe quiz your friends and family, too!

1

What are the three branches of government?
- a. Liberal, conservative, independent
- b. Legislative, executive, judicial
- c. Oak, maple, pine

2

How are changes made to the U.S. Constitution?
- a. By amendments
- b. By decision of the president
- c. By popular vote

3

How many amendments does the U.S. Constitution have?
- a. 10
- b. 27
- c. 50

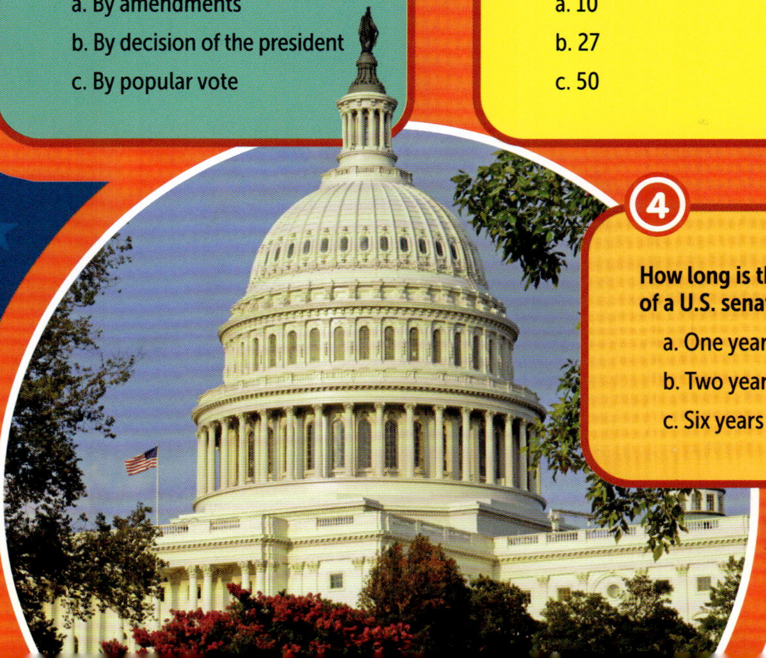

4

How long is the term of a U.S. senator?
- a. One year
- b. Two years
- c. Six years

5
How long is the term for a member of the House of Representatives?
- a. One year
- b. Two years
- c. Six years

6
Some states have more representatives than others. Why?
- a. Because they have more people
- b. Because they are a bigger size
- c. Because they asked nicely

7
Who appoints federal judges?
- a. The Supreme Court
- b. The attorney general
- c. The president

8
How many seats are on the U.S. Supreme Court?
- a. 5
- b. 9
- c. As many as the president wants

9
What does the president's Cabinet do?
- a. Holds the president's favorite books
- b. Hides the president in an emergency
- c. Advises the president

ANSWERS:

1. **b**—Legislative, executive, judicial
2. **a**—By amendments
3. **b**—27
4. **c**—Six years
5. **b**—Two years
6. **a**—Because they have more people
7. **c**—The president
8. **b**—9
9. **c**—Advises the president

Glossary

ADMINISTRATION
the officials who form the executive branch under a president

AMENDMENTS
changes or additions to a constitution

APPEAL
a legal request for one court to review a lower court's decision

APPOINTED
chosen for a government position

ARTICLES OF CONFEDERATION
the document that outlines the first national government of the United States

BALLOT
the piece of paper used to mark a vote, or the listing of all the people running in an election

BICAMERAL
having two separate chambers, or parts, in a legislature

BILL
a proposed law debated in Congress

BUDGET
a government's plan for how much money it will take in and how much it will spend

CABINET
the heads of executive agencies who advise a president and carry out their plans

CANDIDATE
a person running for a political office

CENSUS
a count of the population done every 10 years

CHECKS AND BALANCES
a system to ensure that no one branch of government becomes too powerful

CIA
Central Intelligence Agency

CLASSIFIED
not available to the public

CLOTURE
the process to end a filibuster

CONSTITUTION
a document that defines the beliefs and laws of a country or state

CONSTITUTIONAL
found to be legal under a government's constitution

DELEGATES
people chosen to represent others at a convention

DISTRICT
a geographic area represented by an elected legislator

DUE PROCESS
the legal guarantee that the government will follow the law in judicial matters

ELECTORAL COLLEGE
the body and process through which the country elects its president

EMBASSY
the offices of one country's government in a foreign country

ENACTED
signed a bill into law

EPA
Environmental Protection Agency

EXECUTIVE BRANCH
the part of a government that carries out and enforces laws

EXECUTIVE ORDER
the implied power of the president (not in the Constitution) to give an order with the legal status of a law

FBI
Federal Bureau of Investigation

FEDERAL
a government system with powers shared between states and a national government

FILIBUSTER
the process in the U.S. Senate for delaying a vote on a bill

FORMER FIRST LADY MICHELLE OBAMA

FLOTUS
first lady of the United States

FOUNDERS
the people who wrote the Constitution or were involved in the creation of the United States

GERRYMANDERING
the redrawing of district boundaries to favor one political party over another

HHS
Department of Health and Human Services

HUD
Department of Housing and Urban Development

IMPEACH
to charge a government official with a crime

INAUGURATION
the swearing in of a new president

INCUMBENT
a person who already holds an elected position

181

INITIATIVE
an effort started by voters to pass a law

INTELLIGENCE
information gathered secretly

JUDICIAL BRANCH
the court system in a government

JUSTICES
judges who serve on the U.S. Supreme Court

LANDSLIDE
a huge number of votes for one candidate

LEGISLATIVE BRANCH
the part of a government that makes laws

LEGISLATURE
the lawmaking body of a government

MAJORITY
in a legislative body, the party with at least half the members plus one

MILITIA
an army made up of citizens called out to defend their town or state

NASA
National Aeronautics and Space Administration

NOMINEE
the person a party chooses to run for an elected office

NSA
National Security Agency

OPINION POLLS
questions asked of voters to find their opinions

PAC
political action committee

PLATFORM
the proposed policies of a candidate or political party

POLLS
the place where people go to vote

POPULAR VOTE
the count of all the votes cast in a presidential election

POTUS
president of the United States

PRESS CONFERENCE
a public event at which a government official speaks to many members of the media at once

NASA'S FIRST SPACE SHUTTLE LAUNCH ON APRIL 12, 1981

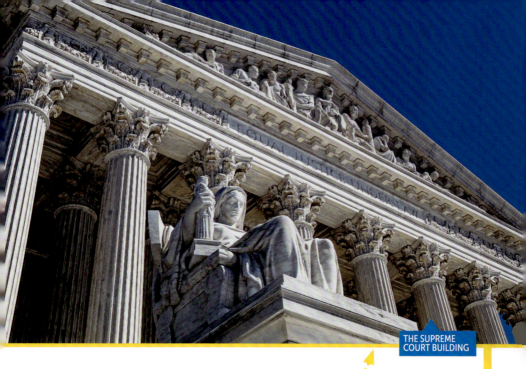

THE SUPREME COURT BUILDING

PROSECUTORS
lawyers who work for a government and bring charges against accused lawbreakers

RATIFY
approve, as a treaty or amendment

RECALL
a vote to see if a government official should be removed from office

REDISTRICTING
a process of redrawing the boundaries of a political district after a census

REFERENDUM
a vote to let people decide an issue

REPEAL
to get rid of a previously approved law or amendment

RUNNING MATE
the person a presidential candidate chooses as their vice presidential candidate

SCOTUS
Supreme Court of the United States

SENIORITY
a position of power based on years of continuous service

SEPARATION OF POWERS
the division of government powers between different branches

SWING STATES
states that don't usually favor one political party or another

TICKET
all the candidates chosen by a political party for an election

USPS
United States Postal Service

VETO
an executive official's power to stop a bill from becoming a law

Boldface indicates illustrations.

Acoustic Kitty (CIA project) 144
Adams, Abigail 13, 92, 93
Adams, John **12**, 19, 34, 51, 56, 57, 75, 92, 93, 96, 103
Adams, John Quincy 34, **34**, 39, 59
Affordable Care Act 143
Air Force One (airplane) 51, **51**, 115
Ali, Muhammad 105, **131**
Aliens, space 109, 147
American Revolution 13, 14, 52, 87, 91, 176
American Samoa, Pacific Ocean 167, **167**
Animal control services 151
Animals: honorary mayors 156–157, **156–157**
Annapolis, Md.: state capital 149, **149**
Arizona 9, 146, 159, 161, 164
Articles of Confederation 14, 15, 41
Astronauts 8, **8**, 46, 104, 131

Bald eagles 177, **177**
Baltimore, Md. 33, 177
Baton Rouge, La: state capital **148**, 148
Bean soup 39
Begin, Menachem 99
Bicameral legislature 30, 133, 167
Biden, Joe 47, 57, **64**, 65, 129, **130**, 157
Bigfoot 8, **8**, 69, 161
Biles, Simone **130**, 131
Bill of Rights 20–21, 22, 23, 34, 133
Bison 176, **176**
Blair, Saira 174, **174**
Bloomers 25, **25**
Bolton, Frances 39, **39**
Bolton, Oliver 39, **39**
Boston, Mass.: state capital 148, **148**

Boucher, Roland 131
Bradley, Bill 47, **47**
Breed, London **153**
Brown v. *Board of Education* (1954) 76, 78
Bureau of Engraving and Printing, Washington, D.C. 107, **107**
Bureau of Indian Affairs 165
Burr, Aaron 57, **57**, 59
Bush, George H. W. 97, 99, 125, **125**
Bush, George W. 59, 60, 110, 115, **115**, 129
Byrnes, James F. 74

Cain, Richard 38, **38**
Calhoun, John C. 45, 133, **133**
California 147, 164; *see also* San Francisco; Yosemite National Park
Camp David, near Thurmont, Md. 98–99, **98–99**
Campaign slogans 118
Caraway, Hattie 45, **45**
Carter, Jimmy 99, 113, **113**, 125, **125**, 135
Castlewood, Va. 147
Caucuses 123
Censuses 30, 31, 37, 69
Central Intelligence Agency (CIA) 51, 73, 107, 109, 144
Charleston, W. Va.: state capitol **132**
Chase, Salmon P. 79, **79**
Cherry trees 87, **87**, 89
Chief Justice of the United States 63, 75, 104
Chisholm, Shirley 34, **34**
Christie, Chris 173
Citizen advisory boards 169
Civics 170
Civil rights movement 89, 117
Civil War, U.S. 17, 39, 44, 52, 76, 130, 131
Claflin, Tennie 117
Claiborne, William Charles Cole 175
Cleveland, Grover 7, **7**, 59, 95, **95**
Cleveland, Ohio 73
Climate change 71, 105, 112, 171
Clinton, Bill 63, 125, **125**, 173
Clinton, Hillary Rodham 9, **9**, 47, **47**, 59, 60, 67, **67**, 127, 129, 157

Cloture 48–49
Colorado
  state pets 170
  see also Denver; Georgetown
Columbus, Christopher 12, 87
Computers 71, 97, 109, 129
Congressional Gold Medal 130, **130**, 165, **165**
Constitutional Convention 14, 16–17, **16–17**
Conventions, political 23, 59, **122**, 123
Coolidge, Calvin 54, 118
Copeny, Mari 171, **171**
Courts, lower
  federal 80–81
  state 138–139
Curtis, Charles 46, **46**

Dayton, Jonathan 14
Debates, presidential 9, **9**, **124**, 124–125, **125**
Debs, Eugene **111**, 117
Declaration of Independence 12, 13, 88, 103
Delaware 151
Delaware Nation 163
Democratic Party 31, 110–113, 129, 133
Denver, Colo.
  alien initiative 147
  public library **150**
Des Moines, Iowa: state capital 149, **149**
Dewey, Thomas 118
Dillon, John F. 142
Dingell, John, Jr. 41
Divorce 27, 133, 139
Douglas, Stephen 125
Douglass, Frederick 91, **91**
Duckworth, Tammy 35, **35**

Eiler, Elsie 153, **153**
Eisenhower, Dwight D. 53, **53**, 95, 99, 118
Election Day 54, 119, 128
Electoral college 24, 39, 58–61
Embassies 68
Eminent domain 145

Enslaved people 11, 17, 20, 24, 52, 96
Enzi, Mike 49
Equal rights amendment (ERA) 27, 34
Exit polls 126

Fair Haven, Vt.: goat mayor 157, **157**
Federal Bureau of Investigation (FBI) 8, 69, 106
Federal Communications Commission 73
Ferraro, Geraldine 113, **113**
Fifth Amendment to the U.S. Constitution 21
Filibusters 48–49
Fillmore, Millard 35, 116
First Amendment to the U.S. Constitution 21, 85, 168
First Ladies 66–67, **66–67**, 105
Flags, U.S. **104**, 105, 176, **176**
Flint, Mich. 171
Fong, Hiram 46, **46**
Ford, Gerald 35, **35**
14th Amendment to the U.S. Constitution 24, 76, 77
Franklin, Benjamin **12**, 14, **14**, 15, 17, 72, 165, 177

George III, King (United Kingdom) 13
Georgetown, Colo.: dog mayor 156, **156**
Gerry, Elbridge 37
Gerrymandering 37
Gettysburg Address 7, 88
Ginsburg, Ruth Bader 79, **79**
Glenn, John 8, **8**, 46
Gore, Al 59, 60, 110, 129
Gore, Thomas P. 47, **47**
Great Depression 27, 45, 53
Great Seal 176, **176**
Greece, ancient 11, 29, 103
Greenbrier (hotel), W. Va. 109
Guam (island), Mariana Islands, Pacific Ocean 167, **167**

Hamilton, Alexander 57, 86, 111, 166
Harris, Kamala **43**, **56**, 57
Harrison, Benjamin 59, 115, **115**
Harrison, William Henry 57, 96
Hawaii 149, 151; see also Pearl Harbor
Hayes, Rutherford B. 39, 59, **59**
Health care 45, 143, 165, 175
Home rule 142, 150
Hope Diamond 105, **105**
Houston, Sam 134, **134**

Illinois: weird law 161
Impeachment 62–63
Independence Day 13
Indian reservations **162**, 162–163, 164
Indiana: state legislature **136**
Initiatives and referendums 146–147
Inouye, Daniel 38, **38**
Interracial marriage 168

J

Jackson, Andrew 47, 59, 65, 112, 133, 175
Jackson, Miss. 149
Japan 35, 53, 76, 87, 89
Jefferson, Thomas
  books 103
  Declaration of Independence **12**, 13
  favorite foods 54
  as governor 135
  Monticello 39
  presidency 34, 39, 59
  quoted 15, 18
  as secretary of state 111
Jefferson City, Mo. 149
Jefferson Memorial, Washington, D.C. 89, **89**
Jelly beans 115, **115**
Jenkins, Albert 26
Jennings, Paul 26
Johnson, Andrew 35, 63
Johnson, Lyndon B. 78, 109

Jousting 158, **158–159**
Judges, election of 140–141
Juries 169

K

Kansas: state fossil 158
Kassebaum, Nancy 45, **45**
Kelly, Mark 46
Kennedy, John F. 45, 47, 64, 125
Kennedy, Robert 64
Kerry, John 129
Key, Francis Scott 177
King, Martin Luther, Jr. 89, 131
Korean War 53
Korematsu, Fred 76, **76**
Korematsu v. *United States* 76

Labranche, Tony 175, **175**
Larrazolo, Octaviano A. 46, **46**
Latin (language) 29
Lawmaking process 82–83
Laws, weird and wacky 160–161
L'Enfant, Pierre Charles 87
LGBTQ Americans 77
Library of Congress, Washington, D.C. 101, **102**, 102–103
Lincoln, Abraham 7, 26, 52, **52**, **88**, 92, 115, **115**, 118, 125

Lincoln, Nebr. 149
Lincoln Memorial, Washington, D.C. 87, 88, **88**, 89
Lloyd, Wesley 27
Lobbying 84–85, 170
Logan Square, Philadelphia, Pennsylvania **168**
Louisiana 150; see also Baton Rouge
Loving v. Virginia 139

Madison, Dolley 96
Madison, James 15, 16, 19, 34, 91, 96, 103
Madison, Wis. 149
Mail-in ballots 129
Maine 59
Marbury v. Madison 75
Marine One (helicopter) 98
Marriage laws 76, 133, 139
Marshall, John 75, 79, **79**
Marshall, Thurgood 78, **78**
Maryland
 laws 144, 147
 official sport 158
 see also Annapolis; Baltimore; Camp David
Mason, George 133, **133**
Massachusetts 136, 145; see also Boston
Mayors, honorary 156–157, **156–157**
Medal of Honor 130, 131
Miller, Lucas Miltiades 27
Mondale, Walter 113
Monroe, James 47, 111
Monticello, Va. 89
Montpelier, Vt. 149
Moon missions 72, 104
Mount Vernon, Va. 66
Murphy, George 44, **44**

National Aeronautics and Space Administration (NASA) 72, 182
National Air and Space Museum, Washington, D.C. 104, **104**
National Archives and Records Administration (NARA) 103
National Mall, Washington, D.C. 86, 87, 88
National Museum of African American History and Culture, Washington, D.C. 104, **104–105**
National Museum of American History, Washington, D.C. **104**, 105
National Museum of Natural History, Washington, D.C. 105, **105**
National Museum of the American Indian, Washington, D.C. 105, **105**
National Security Agency (NSA) 108
National Zoological Park, Washington, D.C. 104
Native Americans 7, 24, 69, 105, 162–165
Nebraska 59, 133, 136, 137
New Deal 53
New Hampshire 122, 134, 136
New Mexico
 history 149
 laws and lawmakers 137, 147
 Navajo lands 164
 official state question 159
 see also Roswell; Santa Fe
New York 38, 85, 120, 175
Newspapers **18**, 18–19, **19**
19th Amendment to the U.S. Constitution 24, 35
Nixon, Richard 47, 63, 77, 94, 125
Nordwall, Adam **162**
North, Wayne 156
North Carolina 45, 159
Northern Mariana Islands, Pacific Ocean 167

Oak trees 177, **177**
Obama, Barack 47, 67, 96, **96**, 113, 121, **124**, 125, 129, 168, **168**, 171
Obama, Michelle 117, **181**
Ocasio-Cortez, Alexandria 113, **113**
O'Connor, Sandra Day 78, **78**, 141
Ohio: statehouse **137**
Oklahoma 163
Omena, Mich.: cat mayor 156, **156**
Oregon 134, 158, 160
Owen, Robert L. 46, **46**

Pacheco, Romualdo 38, **38**
Panama Canal 53
Paxton, Ken 91
Pearl Harbor, Hawaii: bombing of (1941) 35, 53, 76
Pelosi, Nancy **32**, 33
Pence, Mike 124
Pentagon, Arlington, Va. 107, **107**, 109
Perot, Ross 118, 125, **125**
Petitions 147, 168
Philadelphia, Pa.
  Constitutional Convention 15, 16–17, **16–17**
  as former national capital 86
  protest demonstration **168**
  Second Continental Congress 13
Phoenix, Ariz. 149
Plessy v. *Ferguson* (1896) 76
Political action committees (PACs) 120
Political parties 7, 31, 33, 110–117
Polls, opinion 126–127
Presidential Medal of Freedom 130, **130**, 131
Presidents of the United States
  Cabinet 29, 57, 64–65, 68

facts and stats 54–55
favorite foods 54, 94
impeachment 62–63
lawmaking process 82–83
powers and duties 51
presidential succession 65
qualifications 50
salary 51
summer retreat **98**, 98–99, **99**
Primary elections 119, 122–123
Pteranodon 158, **158**
Puerto Rico 166, **166**

Quebec, Canada 15

Rainey, Joseph 38, **38**
Rankin, Jeannette 35, **35**
Reagan, Nancy 67, **67**, 131
Reagan, Ronald 65, 67, 78, 115, **115**, 125, **125**, 130, 135, **135**
Reno, Nev.: weird law 160
Republican Party 31, 110–111, 114–115, 129, 133
Revels, Hiram 45, **45**
Richards, Ann 173
Rome, ancient 29, 42
Romney, Mitt **124**, 125
Roosevelt, Eleanor 66, **66**
Roosevelt, Franklin D. 53, **53**, 66, 83, 98, 113, **113**
Roosevelt, Theodore 10, **10**, 53, **53**, 55, 115, **115**, 116, 176
Roswell, N. Mex. 109

Sadat, Anwar 99
Same-sex marriage 77
San Francisco, Calif. 147, 153
Sanchez, Linda 38, **38**
Sanchez, Loretta 38, **38**
Santa Fe, N. Mex.: state capital **149**

Scalia, Antonin 79, **79**
Schmitt, Harrison 46
Second Continental Congress 13
Secrets, government 108–109
Segregation 76, 117
September 11 attacks (2001) 71, 99, 107
Shallus, Jacob 16
Silly string, laws against 161
Slavery 11, 17, 20, 24, 26, 34, 44, 91, 111
Smithsonian Institution, Washington, D.C.
  museums 104–105, **104–105**
Social Security 53
Socialist Party 111, 117
Sotomayor, Sonia 79, **79**
South Dakota 61, 147
Speaker of the House 32–33, 65
Stadnyk, Landin 175, **175**
"Star-Spangled Banner" (national anthem) 105, 177
State capitols **132**, 148–149, **148–149**
State symbols 158–159, **158–159**
Student governments 172–173
Supreme Court Building, Washington, D.C. 101, 106, **106**
Supreme Court of the United States (SCOTUS) 29, 37, 41, 51, **74**, 74–79, **75**, 163
Sweeney, Robert Augustus 131
Swing states 61, 110

Taxes: colonial America 13
Taylor, Zachary 55, **55**, 94
Tener, John 38
10th Amendment to the U.S. Constitution 21, 133
Terrorism 71, 99, 107
Texas 149, 151, 159
Thomas-Greenfield, Linda **65**
Thurmond, Strom 49
Trail of Tears 163
Tribal nations 105, 162–165, 166
Truman, Harry S. **8**, 47, 98, 113
Trump, Donald 9, **9**, 59, 60, 63, **63**, 127, 129, 157
12th Amendment to the U.S. Constitution 24, 39
25th Amendment to the U.S. Constitution 25, 56
Tyler, John 35

Uncle Sam 177, **177**
U.S. Army 27, 88, 130
U.S. Capitol, Washington, D.C. **28**, **31**, 39, **42**, 87, 96, 100–101, **100–101**, 103
U.S. Congress
  constitutional amendment process 22
  counting electoral votes 59
  House of Representatives 15, 17, 29, 30–39, 175
  impeachment proceedings 62–63
  inside the Capitol 101–102
  lawmaking process 82–83
  and lobbying 84–85
  Senate 8, 15, 17, 29, 42–49
  term limits 40–41
U.S. Constitution
  amendment process 22–23
  background 14–15
  drafting and signing of 16–17, **16–17**
  framework of government 14, 15, 28–29
  judicial review 75
  list of amendments 21, 24–25
  rejected amendments 26–27, 41
  see also Bill of Rights
U.S. Department of Agriculture 64, 69
U.S. Department of Commerce 69
U.S. Department of Defense 68, 107, 108–109
U.S. Department of Education 71
U.S. Department of Energy 71
U.S. Department of Health and Human Services 64, 70
U.S. Department of Homeland Security 71
U.S. Department of Housing and Urban Development 70
U.S. Department of Justice 64, 69
U.S. Department of Labor 70
U.S. Department of the Interior 69, 165
U.S. Department of the Treasury 64, 68
U.S. Department of Transportation 64, 70
U.S. Department of Veterans Affairs 71

U.S. Environmental Protection Agency 73
U.S. Food and Drug Administration 70
U.S. Forest Service 166
U.S. government
  checks and balances 15, 29
  executive branch 15, 29, 50–51, 64–65, 72, 134–135, 173
  judicial branch 15, 28, 74–81, 133
  legislative branch 15, 16, 28, 30–49
  secret programs 108–109
  separation of powers 15, 29
U.S. Navy 125, 130, 131
U.S. Postal Service 72
U.S. Secret Service 51, 71
U.S. Virgin Islands, West Indies 166
Utah 109, 164

Van Buren, Martin 116
Venus flytraps 159, **159**
Veterans, military 35, 67, 71, 151
Vetoes 82, 83
Vice President of the United States 43, 56–57
Vietnam War 34, 117, 165
Virginia
  history 86, 87, 89, 133, 150
  laws 139, 160
  state constitution 169
Voting rights 24, 25, 35

Walker, Mary Edwards 131, **131**
Wallace, George 117
War of 1812 96, **96**, 177
Warren, Earl 76, 78, **78**
Washington, D.C.
  creation of 86–87
  government buildings 106–107, **106–107**
  monuments and memorials 87, **87**, 88–89, **88–89**
  museums 104–105, **104–105**
  statehood question 90–91
  see also Library of Congress; U.S. Capitol;

White House
Washington, George
  Constitutional Convention 15, **17**
  paintings of **52**, 96, 100
  and political parties 110–111
  presidency 19, 52, 64
Washington, Martha 66, **66**
Washington Monument, Washington, D.C. 87, **87**, 88, **88**
Webster, Daniel 44, **44**, 45
White House, Washington, D.C.
  bowling alley 8, **8**, 93
  burning of (1814) 96, **96**
  East Room 93, **93**
  fun facts 94–95
  history 92, 96–97, 115
  Lincoln Bedroom 92, **92**
  movie theater 93
  Oval Office 92, **92**
  Rose Garden 93, **93**
West Wing **92**, 96
Wilson, Woodrow 113, **113**
Woodhull, Victoria 117
World War I 35, 117, 177
World War II 35, 53, 76, 88, 89, 165, 177
World War II Memorial, Washington, D.C. 89, **89**
Wright brothers 104

Yamaguchi, Jeremy 174, **174**
Yosemite National Park, Calif. **135**

Zimmerman, Hannah 175, **175**

PHOTO CREDITS

Unless noted below, illustrations by Josh Lynch; presidential caricatures by Adrian Lubbers. Maps by NG Maps.

AS: Adobe Stock; DR: Dreamstime; GI: Getty Images; LCPPD: Library of Congress Prints and Photographs Division; SS: Shutterstock

Cover (Capitol), Orhan Cam/SS; Spine (background), eMIL'/AS; Back cover (CTR), jreika/AS; 1 (background, throughout), eMIL'/AS; 1, Katia/AS; 2-3 (background), drnadig/E+/GI; 4-5 (background), Olga Moonlight/AS; 4-5 (bunting, throughout), smastepanov2012/AS; 4 (headers, throughout), YULIYA/AS; 6 (LO LE), Krakenimages/AS; 7 (frame, throughout), Kamil Macniak/SS; 7 (CTR), ombre spagla/AS; 8-9 (background, throughout), Natasha_S/AS; 8 (UP LE), Bettmann/GI; 8 (UP RT), NASA; 8 (LO RT), Marion Carpenter/Bettmann/GI; 9 (bunting, throughout), Regormark/AS; 9 (UP), Elena Kharichkina/AS; 9 (CTR), Anastasiia/AS; 9 (LO), John Locher/AP Photo; 10 (UP LE), Mike Powell/The Image Bank/GI; 12 (UP), John Parrot/Stocktrek Images/GI; 12 (LO), Scisetti Alfio/AS; 13 (UP), Brian/AS; 13 (CTR), gearstd/AS; 14 (LO), GraphicaArtis/Archive Photos/GI; 15 (CTR), railwayfx/AS; 16-17 (UP), GraphicaArtis/Archive Photos/GI; 16 (LO LE), Mega Pixel/SS; 18, Scanrail/AS; 19 (UP), terovesalainen/AS; 19 (CTR RT), Rafa Irusta/AS; 19 (LO RT), mikroman6/Moment/GI; 20 (LO), Pixfiction/SS; 21 (background), Andrey_Kuzmin/SS; 21 (UP LE), RuMax/AS; 21 (UP RT), Jojje/SS; 21 (LO RT), 2xSamara/AS; 21 (CTR LE), Mirror Image Studio/AS; 22-23 (stone texture), fivepointsix/AS; 23 (UP RT), Rawpixel/AS; 24-25 (background), Andrey_Kuzmin/SS; 24 (LE), adamkaz/E+/GI; 25 (UP), World History Archive/Alamy Stock Photo; 26 (LO), Djbobus/DR; 27 (UP RT), Heritage Images/Hulton Archive/GI; 27 (UP LE), fStop Images GmbH/Alamy Stock Photo; 27 (CTR LE), VERSUSstudio/SS 27 (LO), kv_san/AS; 28 (UP), turtix/SS; 28 (CTR), Erika Cross/SS; 28 (LO), Brandon Bourdages/SS; 29, akinbostanci/E+/GI; 30 (UP), Chip Somodevilla/GI; 30 (LO), Ermolaev Alexandr/AS; 31 (UP), Keith Lamond/SS; 31 (CTR, throughout), PrimeMockup/AS; 31 (LO RT), Charles Dharapak/AP Photo; 32, Graeme Sloan/AP Photo/Sipa USA; 33 (LO), J Paulson/SS; 34 (UP RT), Michael Tighe/Donaldson Collection/GI; 34 (CTR LE), VCG Wilson/Corbis/GI; 35 (CTR), Bettmann/GI; 35 (LO), Caroline Brehman/CQ Roll Call via AP Images; 36-37 (stone texture), fivepointsix/AS; 37 (LO CTR), Sanja/AS; 37 (LO RT), Sarin Images/Granger, All rights reserved; 38 (UP), The Protected Art Archive/Alamy Stock Photo; 38 (CTR RT), LCPPD; 38 (LO RT), Africa Studio/AS; 38 (CTR), CQ Roll Call via GI; 38 (LO LE), Susan Walsh, File/AP Photo; 38 (CTR LE), Archive PL/Alamy Stock Photo; 39 (UP), colaimages/Alamy Stock Photo; 40-41 (background), Olga Moonlight/AS; 40 (UP), Andrey Burmakin/SS; 40 (LO), razihusin/AS; 41, Prostock-studio/AS; 42 (UP), Official U.S. Senate Photo; 42 (CTR), Universal History Archive/Universal Images Group via GI; 43 (LO), Michael Brochstein/AP Photo/Sipa; 44 (UP), LCPPD; 44 (candy frame), Iuliia Gorshkova/AS; 45 (UP LE), LCPPD; 45 (CTR RT), Chris Martin/CQ Roll Call/GI; 45 (LO LE), LCPPD; 46 (UP RT), Bettmann/GI; 46 (LO RT), LCPPD; 46 (LO CTR), LCPPD; 46 (LO LE), Denis Rozhnovsky/AS; 46 (UP LE), LCPPD; 47 (UP), Bettmann/GI; 47 (CTR LE), Diana Walker/GI; 47 (CTR RT), Valerii Evlakhov/AS; 47 (LO LE), Larry Downing/Reuters; 48 (CTR), VadimGuzhva/AS; 48 (LO), razihusin/AS; 49, Julie Clopper/SS; 50 (UP), OlegAlbinsky/GI; 51 (crown), Hurst Photo/SS; 51 (LO), Nerthuz/SS; 52 (UP RT), Rembrandt Peale/New York Historical Society/Bridgeman Images; 52 (LO LE), LCPPD; 53 (UP RT), LCPPD; 53 (CTR RT), GraphicaArtis/GI; 53 (LO RT), photastic/SS; 53 (CTR LE), Hulton Archive/GI; 54 (UP), U.S. Army/Texas A&M University via GI; 54 (fries), johnfoto18/SS; 54 (mac), gowithstock/SS; 54 (LO LE), Piotr Marcinski/AS; 54 (LO RT), rtsimages/AS; 55 (horse), Erik Lam/SS; 55 (rabbit), Jiang Hongyan/SS; 55 (lizard), ThomasDeco/SS; 55 (pig), Tsekhmister/SS; 55 (guinea), Eric Isselee/SS; 55 (bear), SunnyS/AS; 56, Octavio Jones/Reuters; 57 (UP), Bettmann/GI; 57 (LO), Bill Sikes/AP Photo; 59 (UP), James Steidl/AS; 60 (UP), Scott J. Ferrell/Congressional Quarterly/GI; 60 (LO), razihusin/AS; 61 (UP RT), Erik McGregor/LightRocket via GI; 61 (CTR RT), Mark Makela/GI; 62, LCPPD; 63 (UP), U.S. Congress via GI; 64 (UP), Sarah Silbiger/Bloomberg via GI; 65 (UP RT), AnEduard/SS; 65 (LO), Michael M. Santiago/GI/GI; 66 (UP), LCPPD; 66 (LO), Bettmann/GI; 67 (UP), Harry Langdon/GI; 67 (LO), David Hume Kennerly/GI; 69 (UP RT), Rudi de Groot/AS; 70, Eky Chan/AS; 71 (UP RT), 5second/AS; 71 (LO), mtsaride/AS; 71 (UP LE), leekris/AS; 72 (CTR), dechevm/AS; 72 (LO LE), Everett Historical/SS; 73 (LO CTR), Floortje/E+/GI; 73 (LO LE), Gino Santa Maria/SS; 74 (LO), Carolyn Franks/DR; 75 (UP), Dana Verkouteren via AP; 75 (CTR RT), Stock Montage/GI; 76 (UP), Jack Delano/PhotoQuest/GI; 76 (CTR LE), Gary Fong/San Francisco Chronicle via GI; 77 (UP RT), Margojh/DR; 77 (LO), Drew Angerer/GI; 78 (UP RT), Bachrach/GI; 78 (CTR LE), Cynthia Johnson/GI; 78 (LO RT), Charles Ommanney/GI; 79 (UP LE), Mark Wilson/GI; 79 (CTR RT), Charles Ommanney/GI; 79 (money), Heritage Auctions, Dallas 79 (LO CTR), Erin Schaff-Pool/GI; 80 (LO LE), Comstock/Stockbyte/GI; 81, Stepan Bormotov/AS; 82-83 (stone texture), fivepointsix/AS; 82, RuMax/AS; 84 (LO), Alex/AS; 85 (CTR RT), Pioneer111/DR; 86 (LO LE), Anatolii/AS; 87 (UP), Songquan Deng/SS; 87 (CTR RT), Art Collection 3/Alamy Stock Photo; 88 (UP LE), dibrova/SS; 88 (CTR), Studio Melange/SS; 89 (UP LE), Mihai_Andritoiu/SS; 89 (CTR RT), Jon Bilous/SS; 89 (LO LE), kropic1/SS; 90 (UP), Drew Angerer/GI; 90 (LO), razihusin/AS; 91 (UP), 12ee12/AS; 91 (LO RT), Corbis/GI; 92-93 (background), bodhichita/SS; 92 (UP RT), Jonathan Ernst/Reuters; 92 (LO LE), Bill O'Leary/The Washington Post via GI; 93 (UP LE), Rob Crandall/Alamy Stock Photo; 93 (UP RT), cherylvb/AS; 93 (CTR RT), TriggerPhoto/iStock/GI; 93 (LO RT), Everett Collection Historical/Alamy Stock Photo; 94 (LO LE), Kevin Dietsch-Pool/GI; 94 (UP LE), Peter Wollinga/DR; 95 (UP RT), Africa Studio/AS; 94 (LO RT), BillionPhotos/AS; 95 (CTR LE), Lumos sp/AS; 95 (LO RT), Ingram 96 (CTR), Pixel-Shot/AS; 97 (UP), Bettmann/GI; 97 (CTR), Svetlana Gryankina/AS; 97 (LO), Harvey Georges/AP Photo; 98 (UP), White House Photo by Susan Biddle/AP Photo; 99 (UP), Andrew Harnik/AP Photo; 99 (pins), Photodisc; 99 (racquet), Elnur/AS; 99 (ball), Africa Studio/SS; 100-101 (background), Paul Hakimata/AS; 100 (UP), demerzel21/AS; 100 (CTR LE), jzajic/AS; 100 (LO CTR), Andrea La Corte/DR; 101 (UP LE), Ken Cole/DR; 101 (CTR RT), Al Drago/Reuters; 102,dkfielding/iStock/GI; 104 (UP RT), Luiz Gustavo F Rossi/SS; 104 (CTR LE), f11photo/SS; 104 (LO RT), Pablo Martinez Monsivais/AP Photo; 105 (UP LE), Cvandyke/SS; 105 (CTR RT), Saul Loeb/AFP/GI; 105 (LO RT), SeanPavonePhoto/AS; 105 (CTR LE), Picturemakersllc/DR; 106 (UP), SeanPavonePhoto/AS; 106 (LO LE), Photos BrianScantlebury/SS; 107 (UP), 4kclips/AS; 107 (CTR), Ivan Cholakov/DR; 107 (LO), Andrii A/AS; 109 (CTR RT), sdecoret/SS; 109 (LO RT), Lena_graphics/AS; 111 (UP RT), GraphicaArtis/GI; 111 (CTR RT), Glasshouse Vintage/Universal History Archive/Universal Images Group/GI; 111 (parrot), Ermolaev Alexande/SS; 112 (UP), Kostyantine Pankin/DR; 112 (CTR), Tidarat/AS; 113 (UP RT), Hulton Archive/GI; 113 (CTR RT), LCPPD; 113 (LO RT), Bettmann/GI; 113 (CTR), William B. Plowman/NBC/NBC Newswire/NBCUniversal via GI; 113 (LO LE), LCPPD; 113 (CTR LE), LCPPD; 114 (UP), Constantine Pankin/SS; 114 (LO RT), Kletr/AS; 115 (UP RT), LCPPD; 115 (CTR RT), LCPPD; 115 (LO RT), Paul Richards/AFP/GI; 115 (LO LE), Paul Richards/AFP/GI; 115 (CTR LE), Bettmann/GI; 117 (CTR), Hulton Archives/GI; 117 (CTR RT), Anatolii/AS; 117 (LO LE), Hulton Archive/GI; 118-119 (stone texture), fivepointsix/AS; 118 (CTR LE), Jonathan Wiggs/The Boston Globe via GI; 119 (LO), Chris Hondros/GI; 120 (LO LE), Gresei/AS; 121 (UP), Kena Betancur/AFP via GI; 121 (CTR RT), BillionPhotos/AS; 121 (LO LE), Jim Cole/AP Photo; 122, Michael Robinson-Chavez/The Washington Post via GI; 123 (CTR RT), Art2ur/SS; 123 (LO), Charlie Neibergall/AP Photo; 124 (UP), Mark Wilson/GI; 124 (LO), Alekss/AS; 125 (UP RT), Digital Genetics/SS; 125 (UP CTR), Bettmann/GI; 125 (LO CTR), Mark Cardwell/Reuters; 125 (LO RT), neftali/SS; 126 (CTR), Uros Petrovic/AS; 127 (UP RT), Javier Brosch/SS; 128 (UP), Kena Betancur/AFP via GI; 128 (LO RT), sonsedskaya/AS; 128 (hat), slaved/AS; 128 (bowtie), Jakub Krechowicz/AS; 129 (UP LE), aluxum/iStock/GI; 129 (LO RT), Trinacria Photo/SS; 130 (UP), Saul Loeb/AFP/GI; 130 (LO RT), Tom Williams/CQ-Roll Call, Inc via GI; 131 (UP LE), Greg Mathieson/Mai/GI;131 (UP RT), LCPPD; 131 (LO RT), The Picture Art Collection/Alamy Stock Photo; 131 (LO LE), Chuck Kennedy/MCT/Tribune News Service/GI; 132, SeanPavonePhoto/AS; 133 (UP CTR), Bettmann/GI; 135 (UP RT), AP Photo; 135 (LO LE), Andrew S/SS; 136 (UP), Keith Ridler/AP Photo; 137 (UP), Vitalii Hulai/SS; 137 (CTR), klenger/AS; 137 (LO), Nagel Photography/SS; 138 (UP), sirtravelalot/SS; 139 (UP RT), Africa Studio/AS; 139 (CTR RT), Bettmann/GI; 139 (LO LE), Comstock/Stockbyte/GI; 140 (UP), Trong Nguyen/DR; 140 (LO), razihusin/AS; 141 (LO RT), zendograph/AS; 142 (UP), littleny/AS; 142 (CTR LE), ActionGP/AS; 143 (UP RT), Ground Picture/SS; 143 (CTR RT), Spiroview Inc./AS; 143 (LO), Miroslav Liska/DR; 144 (LO), igorkol_ter/AS; 145 (UP LE), lerm90/AS; 145 (UP CTR), thaporn942/AS; 145 (hand), jorgecachoh/AS; 145 (car), Whitevector/SS; 145 (LO RT), geargodz/AS; 145 (LO LE), Kadmy/AS; 147 (UP RT), Acey Harper/GI; 147 (LO RT), Tranz2d/DR; 147 (LO LE), Svetlana Foote/SS; 148 (UP), Sean Pavone/DR; 148 (LO), Ball Studios/AS; 149 (UP LE), Sean Pavone/SS; 149 (CTR RT), Jacob/AS; 149 (LO LE), Sergey Novikov/AS; 150, Peter Gridley/GI; 151 (UP RT), prescott09/AS; 152-153 (UP), Michael Macor/San Francisco Chronicle via GI; 152 (LO LE), Piotr Marcinski/AS; 152 (hat), Victor Moussa/AS; 153 (LO LE), Elnur/AS; 153 (LO RT), Rick Wilking/Reuters; 154 (UP), alexeys/iStock/GI; 154 (CTR LE), Eric Isselée/AS; 154 (LO RT), auimeesri/AS; 155 (UP), Josh Lynch; 155 (LO RT, LO LE), KonstantinPetkov/AS; 155 (LO CTR), marilyn barbone/AS; 156 (UP RT), Dustin Schaefer/Official Snow Dog; 156 (CTR LE), Kanda McKee; 156 (LO RT), Stephanie North; 157 (CTR RT), sommai/AS; 157 (LO RT), Sabrina Allen/AS; 158 (UP), Captain Wang/SS; 158 (CTR), Perytskyy/AS; 158 (LO), Victor Moussa/AS; 159 (UP RT), SunnyS/AS; 159 (peppers), ChaoticDesignStudio/AS; 159 (CTR LE), Troy Aossey/Stone/GI; 159 (LO), Mara Fribus/AS; 160 (UP), nd700/AS; 160 (CTR LE), cynoclub/AS; 160 (LO RT), fergregory/AS; 161 (UP RT), Paul Brady Photography/SS; 161 (UP LE), Tsekhmister/SS; 161 (CTR LE), Simon/AS; 161 (LO), Tim UR/AS; 162 (UP), Terry Pierson/The Press-Enterprise via GI; 162 (Nez Perce), Joe Sohm/Visions of America/Universal Images Group via GI; 162 (Navajo), Walter Bibikow/Digital Vision/GI; 163, Sarin Images/Granger, All rights reserved; 164 (UP), aiisha/AS; 164 (LO LE), Oleksii/AS; 165 (CTR RT), Corbis/GI; 165 (LO RT), Chip Somodevilla/GI; 166 (UP RT), railway fx/SS; 166 (LO), SeanPavonePhoto/AS; 167 (UP LE), Khaled/AS; 167 (UP RT), Oleksii/AS; 167 (LO RT), sezerozger/AS; 167 (LO CTR), michaelfitz/AS; 167 (CTR LE), Peto/AS; 168 (UP), Cory Clark/NurPhoto via GI; 168 (LO LE), Joseph Sohm/SS; 169 (UP RT), Roy Grogan/AS; 169 (LO LE), Jason/AS; 170 (LO LE), Ermolaev Alexandr/AS; 171 (UP LE), Alessandro Biascioli/iStock/GI; 171 (UP RT), Steve Perez/Detroit News via AP; 171 (CTR RT), geargodz/AS; 171 (LO LE), Hill Street Studios/Digital Vision/GI; 172 (UP), Krakenimages/AS; 172 (LO LE), Svitlana/AS; 173 (UP), Bob Daemmrich/Alamy Stock Photo; 174 (UP), Cliff Owen/AP Photo; 174 (LO), Glenn Koenig/Los Angeles Times via GI; 175 (UP RT), Tony Labranche; 175 (CTR LE), Derrick L. Turner/Michigan State University Communications; 175 (LO LE), Martha Stewart/Harvard Kennedy School; 176 (UP RT), Grey Mountain Photo/SS; 176 (LO LE), Digital Media Pro/SS; 176 (LO RT), sassy1902/E+/GI; 177 (UP LE), Arak7/DR; 177 (UP RT), KonstantinPetkov/AS; 177 (CTR RT), Kevin Mazur/WireImage/GI; 177 (LO), emranashraf/AS; 178, Orhan Çam/AS; 179 (UP), Alexstar/AS; 179 (LO), InputUX/AS; 180, Janece Flippo/SS; 181, LCPPD; 182, Everett Historical/SS; 183, David/AS; 186, AR Pictures/SS; 188, U.S. Army/Texas A&M University via GI; 192 (LO RT), sonsedskaya/AS; 192 (hat), slaved/AS; 192 (bowtie), Jakub Krechowicz/AS

CREDITS

Dedicated to all the hardworking staffers at all levels who help our elected officials and keep governments running. —MB

Copyright © 2024 National Geographic Partners, LLC. All rights reserved. Reproduction of the whole or any part of the contents without written permission from the publisher is prohibited.

NATIONAL GEOGRAPHIC and Yellow Border Design are trademarks of the National Geographic Society, used under license.

Since 1388, the National Geographic Society has funded more than 14,000 research, conservation, education, and storytelling projects around the world. National Geographic Partners distributes a portion of the funds it receives from your purchase to National Geographic Society to support programs including the conservation of animals and their habitats. To learn more, visit natgeo.com/info.

For more information, visit nationalgeographic.com, call 1-877-873-6846, or write to the following address:

National Geographic Partners, LLC
1145 17th Street NW
Washington, DC 20036-4688 U.S.A.

For librarians and teachers: nationalgeographic.com/books/librarians-and-educators

More for kids from National Geographic: natgeckids.com

For rights or permissions inquiries, please contact National Geographic Books Subsidiary Rights: bookrights@natgeo.com

Designed by Girl Friday Productions, LLC

Library of Congress Cataloging-in-Publication Data

Names: Burgan, Michael, author.
Title: Weird but true know-it-all U.S. government / Michael Burgan.
Other titles: Weird but true know-it-all United States government
Description: Washington, D.C. : National Geographic Kids, 2024. | Includes index. | Audience: Ages 8-12 | Audience: Grades 4-6
Identifiers: LCCN 2022036867 | ISBN 9781426375279 (paperback) | ISBN 9781426375347 (library binding)
Subjects: LCSH: United States--Politics and government--Juvenile literature
Classification: LCC JK40 .B875 2024 | DDC 320.473--dc23/eng/20220914
LC record available at https://lccn.loc.gov/2022036867

Acknowledgments
The publisher would like to thank the team that made this book: Ariane Szu-Tu, editor; Sanjida Rashid, design director; Sarah J. Mock, senior photo editor; Professor Robert D. Johnston of the history program at the University of Illinois at Chicago for his expert review; Carrie Wicks, copy editor; Abigail Bass, fact-checker; and Nicole Overton and Randall R. Murphy, J.D., for their sensitivity reviews.

The publisher would also like to thank Peter Brown for his expert review of the manuscript.

Printed in China
23/RRDH/1